WOMEN
— *of* —
MYTH

From
**DEER WOMAN and MAMI WATA
to AMATERASU and ATHENA,**
Your Guide to the Amazing and Diverse
Women from World Mythology

JENNY WILLIAMSON and **GENN MCMENEMY**
Creators of the *Ancient History Fangirl* Podcast

Illustrated by **SARA RICHARD** with a Foreword by **LIV ALBERT**

Adams Media
NEW YORK LONDON TORONTO SYDNEY NEW DELHI

Adams Media
An Imprint of Simon & Schuster, LLC
100 Technology Center Drive
Stoughton, Massachusetts 02072

First Adams Media hardcover edition February 2023

ADAMS MEDIA and colophon are trademarks of Simon & Schuster.

For information about special discounts for bulk purchases, please contact Simon & Schuster Special Sales at 1-866-506-1949 or business@simonandschuster.com.

The Simon & Schuster Speakers Bureau can bring authors to your live event. For more information or to book an event contact the Simon & Schuster Speakers Bureau at 1-866-248-3049 or visit our website at www.simonspeakers.com.

Interior design by Sylvia McArdle
Illustrations by Sara Richard

Manufactured in China

10 9 8 7 6 5 4 3 2

Library of Congress Cataloging-in-Publication Data
Names: Williamson, Jenny, author. | McMenemy, Genn, author. | Richard, Sara, illustrator.
Title: Women of myth / Jenny Williamson and Genn McMenemy, Creators of the Ancient History Fangirl Podcast, Illustrated by Sara Richard.
Description: Stoughton, Massachusetts: Adams Media, 2023 | Includes index.
Identifiers: LCCN 2022014641 | ISBN 9781507219416 (hc) | ISBN 9781507219423 (ebook)
Subjects: LCSH: Women--Mythology. | Women's studies.
Classification: LCC BL325.F4 W55 2023 | DDC 202/.13082--dc23/eng/20220512
LC record available at https://lccn.loc.gov/2022014641

ISBN 978-1-5072-1941-6
ISBN 978-1-5072-1942-3 (ebook)

DEDICATION

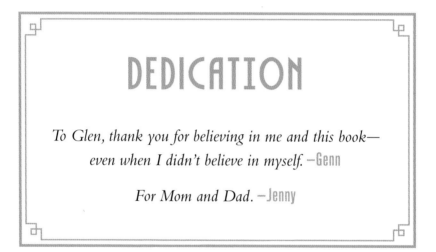

To Glen, thank you for believing in me and this book—
even when I didn't believe in myself. −Genn

For Mom and Dad. −Jenny

ACKNOWLEDGMENTS

It's still such an unreal dream that this book exists. We wrote the proposal for this book together after not seeing each other due to the pandemic for over two years. We sat at a little outdoor restaurant in Athens, typing on our laptops and furiously researching and suggesting different women to feature in this book. And that process still feels like a dream. We were told our proposal for this book was going to be accepted for publication at the ruins of the ancient Minoan palace, Knossos, in Crete. Everything that's happened since has felt a little like a myth to us. Thank you so much for purchasing this book. Thank you for taking this journey with us.

This book would not have been possible without so many people. We are probably going to forget someone, so we're apologizing in advance. Our infinite thanks go out to:

Our amazing editor Rebecca Tarr Thomas—thank you for this incredible project and your belief in us. We are so grateful to tell these stories and to work with you.

Our development editor, Laura Daly, for the best notes, guidance, and keeping us ruthlessly on task—thank you.

The amazing team at Adams Media and Simon & Schuster for marketing, producing, publicizing, and selling this book.

The incredible Liv Albert. It's safe to say this book wouldn't exist without you. Your friendship throughout a global pandemic, your advice, your wicked sense of humor, and your grace have been some of the best gifts the last few years have given us. Thank you for being not just a friend, but an epic friend. Here's to more Spartacus Mondays and cocktails in Greece.

The brilliant classics, Mediterranean studies, and history podcast communities online. Thank you so much for your support and your belief in us. Getting to know you all has been one of the best things about starting our podcast.

The amazing authors who have given us their support, advice, and encouragement. Your support has meant the world to us. Thank you so much to Nikita Gill, Jennifer Saint, Elodie Harper, Ben Aaronovitch, Mike Duncan, and Joanne Harris.

Our wonderful listeners of the *Ancient History Fangirl* podcast. Thank you for letting us tell you all the dirt from the ancient world. For giving us a place in your lives. And for all the kind words you've shared with us on social media and via email.

Genn would also like to thank the following people:

To my mother, the keeper of all the best stories, who introduced me to mythology and reading and who never gets tired of my telling her random snippets of history and lore. And to my father, who can spin a tale like no one else—I am pretty sure all my storytelling comes from listening to your stories about dinosaurs hiding around the treetops, just out of sight. To my brothers—Pat, who can tell a story and make me laugh with just two words (cool beans!), and Greg, who has been known to spin the truth into fiction. And to my sister-in-law, Jen, whose support has never failed—thank you!

To my incredible friends Angel and Porsche, thank you for the late-night phone calls, the life advice, and all the support you've given me. I am truly lucky to call you friends and family.

To my niece, Elizabeth, and my honorary nieces—Lucy, Claire, and Sophie—I hope you find women in this book who inspire you.

To the Movie Club (Dan, Nikki, Curtis, Lou, Pat, Jen, and Anne)—which started on FaceTime as a way to get through the pandemic and check in on each other weekly and turned into lifelong friends. Thank you for forcing me outside of my comfort zone and cheering on this book!

To my creative partner, Jenny. There is no one I'd rather be on this crazy adventure with. Thank you for always helping me find the story, for texting me random mythology facts at ungodly hours, and for helping me find my way out of the deep, dark woods and onto the beach of everything I've always wanted. I'm beyond lucky to have you as a friend and work wife. Here's to more books and more adventures.

And last, but never least, to my husband. The past few years have been difficult for us—from surviving a global pandemic to caring for a dying family member. We lost your dad before this book was finished, but I know he would have loved it. Thank you, Glen, for believing in me and this book even when I didn't. For always reminding me that this book and my dreams were worth fighting for. And for sending our tiny dog, Triss, to scratch at the shed at just the right moments for cuddles and walkies. I love you.

Jenny would also like to thank the following people:

Thank you to my mom, who ran the library in the small town where I grew up and who let me hide in the stacks for as long as I wanted. That library was my first doorway into the amazing worlds of mythology and history that I still escape to today.

Thank you to my dad, whose endless support and love have kept me afloat and who taught me to love history and story as much as he does.

Thank you to my dear friends, to Juliet and Amanda and Brittney and Joe and Amy and Jayel and Lynsey and Angel, who have endlessly believed in me and listened to my going on and *on* about history and mythology over cocktails, who have encouraged my obsessions and cheered me on in this journey.

And, of course, thank you to Genn, whose heart and imagination are both boundless, who makes all our creative endeavors better and stronger and more electric, who is always there for a 3 a.m. text convo about Dionysus, and without whom this book and our podcast and my life as I know it would not exist. I love you. Thanks for spinning our dreams into reality with me.

CONTENTS

HEROINES ... ١٠١

PART 3:

MONSTERS ... 181

FOREWORD

By Liv Albert
Host of *Let's Talk About Myths, Baby!* Podcast

————— ◆ —————

There's nothing I love more than mythology…except maybe *women in mythology*. Ancient mythologies tell us so much about the ancient people who developed and believed in them—the good and the bad. Myths explain the natural world and give order to otherwise random and chaotic phenomena. Myths connect humanity with the divine, telling stories of gods and heroes with humanizing characteristics. Myths can be insightful, beautiful, tragic, funny, or even some kind of incredible melding of all of these themes. Myths are timeless and invaluable. (Did I mention there's nothing I love more than mythology?)

As the host of the podcast *Let's Talk About Myths, Baby!* and an author specializing in women of Greek mythology, I am always seeking to further my knowledge of mythologies beyond the Greek. Pop culture and reception today disproportionately favor the classical mythology of Greece and Rome, leaving the rest of the world's mythologies by the wayside. But understanding the importance and relevance of ancient peoples and their mythologies beyond those of Europe is vital, as is looking at the ways those ancient peoples understood the fluidity and spectrum of gender. Fortunately, in *Women of Myth*, my dear friends Jenny Williamson and Genn McMenemy have created the perfect primer for learning about the vast and vibrant women of world mythologies. Alongside their words, Sara Richard has created a stunning and diverse means of visualizing those women. This book fills a gaping hole in the realm of mythological anthologies, giving voices and faces to some of the most fascinating and incredible women of world mythology.

For so long, retellings of mythologies have focused on the men: gods, heroes, and traditionally masculine warriors, while giving the women alongside them little credit. Meanwhile, the actual mythologies have always had great respect for their goddesses and heroines, even their so-called "monstrous" female-assigned creatures—that respect often just didn't trickle down through the fog of patriarchal values to reach us today. In *Women of Myth*, Jenny and Genn examine women of mythologies the world over, providing lesser-known insights into even the most famous of goddesses and heroines, and amplifying the stories of others rarely mentioned in popular mythological anthologies. Just as they do in their fun and accessible podcast, *Ancient History Fangirl*, Jenny and Genn take special care with the stories of these women, doing their best to look beyond the traditional Western lens, and give the women their own voices. From Amaterasu to Ishtar and Kali to Mami Wata, *Women of Myth* is here to introduce you to all your new favorite goddesses.

INTRODUCTION

ATARGATIS, the Syrian mermaid goddess who inspired a slave rebellion.

THÁKANE, a southern African dragon slayer and monster hunter.

AMATERASU, the powerful Japanese goddess of the heavens and the sun.

———◆◆———

The women of mythology are an awe-inspiring and formidable group from around the world whose stories will leave you amazed, impressed, inspired, and even shocked. In *Women of Myth*, you'll meet fifty of these remarkable women, representing cultures from Aztec to Zulu.

These profiles highlight the women's backgrounds and famous parts of their stories, plus a list of alternative names they're known by; a description of their appearance; and any animals, magical objects, or other symbols they're associated with—when we had access to that information. You'll marvel at the incredible range of these women's abilities, from the Egyptian goddess Isis's focus on magic and healing to the brave leadership of Triệu Thị Trinh, a 9-foot-tall Vietnamese heroine who rode an elephant into battle. The book divides their stories into three main categories:

- **Mighty goddesses:** Some of these women represent the power of the natural world—such as Pele, the volcano and creation goddess; Oya, the goddess of storms and winds; and Mami Wata, a formidable water goddess. Others are goddesses of sex and sexual agency—they know what they want, they aren't afraid to be the pursuer, and their sexuality refuses to be bound by the patriarchy. Still others are strong warrior goddesses who stalk the battlefield, sorceresses who master the magical arts and the powers of prophecy, or deities who represent the destructive powers of transformation and change.

- **Bold heroines:** These heroines are warriors, healers, mothers, sorceresses, and storytellers. They fight against oppression, lead their people, defy their husbands, get revenge, establish new cities, and protect their families and communities. (Think of Atalanta, the Greek heroine who hunted the Calydonian boar and joined the famous Argonauts.) Some of our heroines present as traditionally feminine; others are more masculine presenting. Some are genderqueer, and many defy conventional gender roles as defined by their cultures.

- **Formidable monsters:** Women labeled "monsters" often tell us more about their cultures' fears, insecurities, and challenges than about the women themselves. Some of these women share warnings, such as the message of the Qalupalik—an Inuit monster—for children not to walk too far out on the ice. A few, such as La Llorona and Aicha Kandicha, speak of underlying tensions between Indigenous cultures and the forces of colonization. Some "monsters," like Deer Woman and Medusa, take power back and right wrongs done against women.

The stunning illustrations alongside some of the profiles can help you envision their mighty prowess. Though many of these women—whether goddess, heroine, or monster—are described as "beautiful" in their original tales, these women are actually much more complex than that one word implies. While we often chose to keep this descriptor to stay true to their original depiction, we also wanted to better capture their multilayered personalities and talents—and emphasize that "beauty" can be very diverse. We asked our incredible artist, Sara Richard, to create illustrations that celebrate their power and beauty in a variety of ways—including diversity of size, body type, gender expression, and skin tone—and get beyond a traditional (Western) ideal of what "beautiful" is.

It's important to note that while some of these stories are folklore, others represent religious beliefs and traditions that are still very active today. We used the term "mythology" to apply broadly to any tale of a supernatural or fantastical nature, but a number of these goddesses, heroines, and monsters are part of current religions—some with millions of believers.

This work honors women in mythology, religion, and folklore around the world—both well-known favorites and ones that are likely new to us. Even though these stories originate from a wide variety of cultures, you'll see common threads of strength, intelligence, community, and inventiveness woven throughout. It's time for these larger-than-life women to enjoy their rightful place in the pantheon of mythical characters that leave us mere mortals fascinated, spellbound, and awestruck.

A NOTE ABOUT THE PRONUNCIATIONS

We have made an attempt to provide pronunciation guides to help people pronounce names they may be unfamiliar with. We chose to provide pronunciations for almost all the names—not just the ones that we thought would be unfamiliar to a Western audience. (We didn't provide pronunciations for those whose names are translated as common English words.)

However, it's important to keep in mind that these pronunciations are not perfect. Some names—such as "Arianrhod" and "Triệu Thị Trinh"—have sounds that are difficult to reproduce in English. Many pronunciations vary due to regional and dialectical language differences. We encourage you to do your own research if you aren't sure and defer to native language speakers if their pronunciation varies from ours.

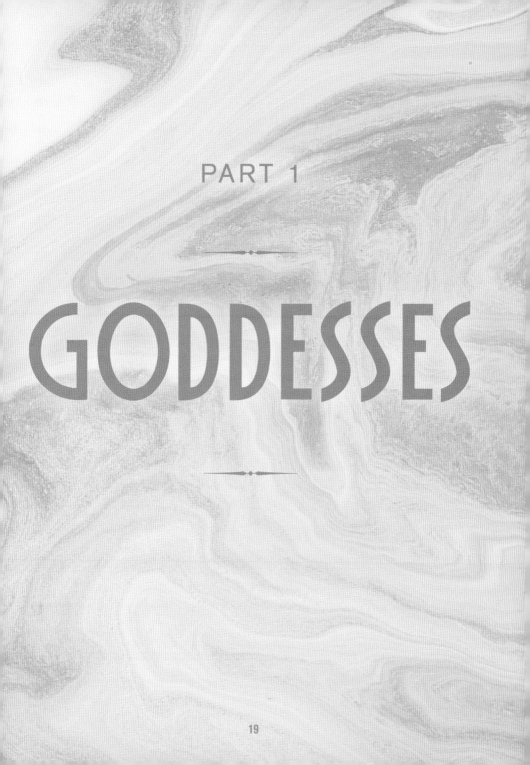

PART 1

GODDESSES

AMATERASU

Japanese Goddess of the Heavens and the Sun

———◆———

PRONUNCIATION: a-ma-te-RA-su

AKA: Amaterasu-ōmikami ("the Great and Glorious Kami Who Illuminates from Heaven"), Ōhirume-no-muchi-no-kami ("the Great Sun of the Kami"); for reference, a "kami" is a god or spirit

APPEARANCE: Amaterasu is said to glow as brightly as the sun.

SYMBOLS:

• Roosters: Roosters are associated with the dawn and the sun. These birds are sacred to Amaterasu and herald her appearance.

• Ravens: They are the messengers of Amaterasu. Their arrival means that she is sending a message.

• Octagonal mirrors: These are significant to Amaterasu, as shown in her story and represented by the Yata-no-Kagami.

• The Imperial Regalia of Japan: The treasures of the Imperial Regalia of Japan all have a place in Amaterasu's legend. These include the Yata-no-Kagami (the Eight-Span Mirror), the Yasakani-no-Magatama (the Grand Jewel), and the Kusanagi-no-Tsurugi (the Grass-Cutting Sword).

• The rising sun: Amaterasu is associated with the rising sun and is also featured on the flag of Japan. The red sun in the center is said to represent her.

———◆———

Overview

Amaterasu is one of the "Three Precious Children" born to the creator god Izanagi after he returned from the underworld seeking purification. The story goes that after Izanagi's wife, Izanami, died in childbirth, the god was so distraught that he went to the underworld to retrieve her.

But Izanami had already eaten the food of the underworld and wasn't allowed to leave. She begged Izanagi to wait for her at the gate of the underworld and give her some time to sort out getting permission to leave, but he instead followed her and noticed her decaying body and flesh. He was so horrified that he returned to the world, seeking purification.

He bathed in a river, and three new kami, or gods, were born. The firstborn was Amaterasu, the most radiant and powerful of the three. She was the sun and became ruler of the heavens. Second was her brother Tsukuyomi. He was the god of the moon, and he was less radiant than his sister—he was only a reflection of her light. He also became her lover. The third child was Susanoo. He had a stormy nature and became the god of the seas and storms.

Amaterasu is a goddess of creation, placed at the center of ancient Shinto and Japanese life and culture. She is the most powerful of all the gods, and you can even see her symbol on the Japanese flag—the rising sun.

In modern times, you can find Amaterasu across lots of pop culture mediums, including video games like *Ōkami* and *SMITE*, manga such as *Naruto* and *Urusei Yatsura*, novels such as *Giles Goat-Boy*, TV shows such as *Stargate SG-1*, and the Yu-Gi-Oh! card game—where she is one of the most powerful cards in the game.

What's Her Story?

Sources vary on the most famous story of Amaterasu, but most of them agree that Amaterasu and her brother Susanoo were engaged in a competition to see who could create better children. They each reproduced asexually. According to some sources, Amaterasu won this competition—either legitimately by producing the "better" children, or through trickery.

Either way, Susanoo lost…and he didn't take it well. He got so angry that he went on a rampage and began destroying the world. Amaterasu was so despondent with the destruction their competition had wrought that she hid herself away in a cave.

With Amaterasu gone, the world was plunged into darkness. The other gods tried to coax Amaterasu out of the cave, but it didn't work—no matter how they pleaded, Amaterasu refused to come out. So all the gods got together and created an epic plan.

The plan went like this: The gods rounded up all the roosters and brought them outside Amaterasu's cave, trying to trick the goddess into thinking the dawn had come (because roosters always crow with the rising sun). They placed a sakaki tree outside the cave's entrance and decorated it with sparkling jewels, white clothes, and a large octagonal mirror at the center to create an illusion of the light of dawn.

Then Amenouzume, the goddess of the dawn, joy, and mirth, did a showstopping striptease. She danced, bare breasted, and all the other gods laughed and cheered and were having a fantastic time watching this show.

Amaterasu was very curious about what was going on outside her cave. She peeked her head out and immediately saw herself reflected in the mirror—and was transfixed by her own beauty and radiance. She also saw Amenouzume's body, we imagine, and was probably transfixed by that as well. The gods told her that she couldn't hide any longer and showed her that the earth needed her. Amaterasu agreed and returned to her position as ruler of the heavens.

It is thought this story might have been used to explain the first solar eclipse in ancient Japan. Amaterasu's disappearance into the cave might have been used to explain solar eclipses, where the sun is briefly blocked by the moon but will return again, just as Amaterasu did.

THE IMPERIAL REGALIA OF JAPAN

According to the legends surrounding Japan's imperial family, their lineage and right to rule goes all the way back to Amaterasu. Amaterasu is so important to the imperial lineage that their regalia all feature symbols of the goddess. There are three items of sacred regalia associated with the imperial family of Japan:

1. The Yata-no-Kagami, or Eight-Span Mirror, is kept in a shrine in Mie Prefecture in Japan—at least theoretically. It may have been destroyed in a fire over a thousand years ago, and since the public does not have access to the regalia, this is hard to verify. The Yata-no-Kagami represents the mirror that was used to lure Amaterasu out of the cave.

2. The Yasakani-no-Magatama, or Grand Jewel, is said to be part of a necklace given to Amaterasu by her father.

3. The Kusanagi-no-Tsurugi, or Grass-Cutting Sword, is believed to have been Susanoo's sword initially. It was later given to Amaterasu.

These reminders of this powerful goddess in the ancient emblems of imperial Japan show how important the legacy of Amaterasu has been throughout the ages, and continues to be today.

ARIANRHOD

Star Goddess of *The Mabinogion*

PRONUNCIATION: ahr-ee-ON-rhod

AKA: Aranrhod, Arianrod, Silver Wheel, the Goddess of the Silver Wheel, the Silver Wheel That Descends Into the Sea

APPEARANCE: Arianrhod is usually depicted as fair-haired and pale.

SYMBOLS:

• **The wheel:** Arianrhod is associated with wheels as a symbol of time and cycles, representing the cycle of the year.

• **Owls:** Arianrhod can change her form into an owl and uses this form to see at night and judge the dead.

• **The moon and North Star:** Arianrhod is a goddess of the moon and associated with the North Star.

Overview

Arianrhod is a complex and fascinating goddess from Welsh mythology. Her story gives us glimpses of a people caught between an ancient Celtic way of life and colonizing Christianity. Arianrhod's story first appears in the Fourth Branch of *The Mabinogion*, one of the earliest written prose stories in Britain—originally written down around the twelfth century A.D. It is based on oral legends that are probably much older.

Written versions of Arianrhod's story come to us through a Christian lens, which sanitizes and chastises Arianrhod for her decisions and lifestyle. However, it is clear that she had a larger role to play as a major goddess in the ancient Celtic religion than these few written stories would make it seem.

Arianrhod was the daughter of Dôn, an ancient Welsh mother goddess. Arianrhod was a fiercely independent woman who lived in a moving castle by the sea, with only female attendants. She had a proclivity for mermen, and they frequently visited her castle, where Arianrhod entertained them at her leisure.

For a while, Arianrhod was free and happy. But all that changed when there was a scandal in the court of King Math, Arianrhod's uncle.

What's Her Story?

Arianrhod lived at her magical moving castle, Caer Arianrhod, located in the Corona Borealis (the northern constellation) and also in Wales—geography is fuzzy here. She had no interest in her uncle Math's court; she was busy entertaining mermen and being the goddess of rebirth, fertility, and the moon. She was also a consummate weaver and spinner. She had power over the wheel that spins the world and was in charge of judging the dead and of reincarnation.

King Math had a very odd *tynged*, or magical prohibition: He had to keep his foot in the lap of a virgin at all times when he was not at war. While this sounds incredibly odd, this *tynged* is actually rooted in the way power was once passed down through Welsh kings.

Prior to Christianity's presence in Wales, the right to rule was passed down matrilineally (essentially, women always held the throne). Through the Christian lens, this got reinterpreted as women being a *literal* throne—an object that holds the feet of the king. So this foot fetish *tynged* was actually about King Math's being granted the right to rule from the women of his country.

Arianrhod's brothers Gwydion and Gilfaethwy were both high-ranking members of Uncle Math's court. Gwydion was a bard, trickster, and powerful magician. His brother Gilfaethwy fell violently in lust with King Math's beautiful lap virgin Goewin. She wanted nothing to do with him, however, and since she was always with King Math—because of the foot-holding thing—Gilfaethwy had no chance of getting a moment alone with her.

So Gilfaethwy went to his brother Gwydion and begged him for help getting Goewin alone. Gwydion obliged his brother by orchestrating a war between the kingdom of Math and that of his archrival, King Pryderi, by stealing Pryderi's otherworldly pigs. King Math was forced to go to war and leave Goewin behind.

While the king was gone, Gilfaethwy raped Goewin. When Math returned, he was furious. First, he married Goewin himself to save her the "shame" of having been raped. And then, since he was a powerful magician, he punished his nephews by turning them into three different pairs of mating animals—elk, cows, and wolves. Each time Gilfaethwy and Gwydion transformed into a new animal, Gwydion had sex with his brother and Gilfaethwy was forced to bear a child. In total, the brothers had three sons, whom Math took and raised as his own.

Eventually, Math decided the brothers had been punished enough and turned them back into human men. Gwydion, perhaps seeking to ingratiate himself, noticed that Math still hadn't found a new virgin to hold his feet in her lap. So Gwydion suggested his sister Arianrhod.

Arianrhod had no desire to be a virgin foot holder, but Gwydion convinced her to go to her uncle's castle anyway—probably under false pretenses. When she arrived, Gwydion devised a test to make sure that Arianrhod was a virgin, which involved stepping over a bent "wand." ("Wand" here is both a literal wand and alludes to a certain bit of male genitalia.)

The second she stepped over the wand, she gave birth to two sons. One was Dylan, probably the son of a merman or sea god. Dylan ran away to the sea when his uncle tried to baptize him. The other child was an amorphous blob. Gwydion hid it in a chest and used his magic to nurture it until it grew into a human boy.

Arianrhod never forgave Gwydion for forcing her to step over the bent wand and give birth. She swore she would never give her son (the amorphous blob one) a name or allow him to take up arms or have a wife—denying him the trappings of manhood. Gwydion managed to circumvent Arianrhod's curses, and the unnamed boy became Lleu Llaw Gyffes, "the Fair-Haired One with the Skilled Hands."

Arianrhod returned to her castle, where she resumed spinning the wheel that turns the world, judging the dead, being the goddess of the moon, and hanging out with mermen. Her castle has been identified as a rock formation westward of Llandwrog in northwest Wales that is visible at low tide.

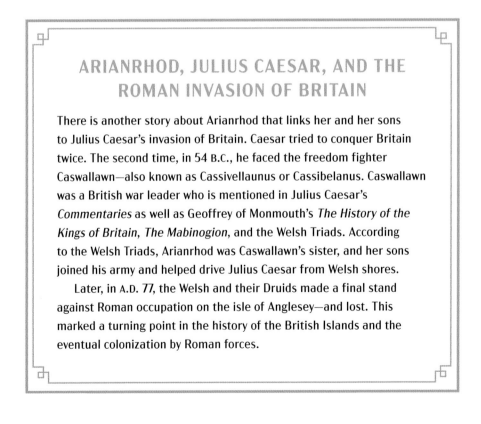

ARIANRHOD, JULIUS CAESAR, AND THE ROMAN INVASION OF BRITAIN

There is another story about Arianrhod that links her and her sons to Julius Caesar's invasion of Britain. Caesar tried to conquer Britain twice. The second time, in 54 B.C., he faced the freedom fighter Caswallawn—also known as Cassivellaunus or Cassibelanus. Caswallawn was a British war leader who is mentioned in Julius Caesar's *Commentaries* as well as Geoffrey of Monmouth's *The History of the Kings of Britain*, *The Mabinogion*, and the Welsh Triads. According to the Welsh Triads, Arianrhod was Caswallawn's sister, and her sons joined his army and helped drive Julius Caesar from Welsh shores.

Later, in A.D. 77, the Welsh and their Druids made a final stand against Roman occupation on the isle of Anglesey—and lost. This marked a turning point in the history of the British Islands and the eventual colonization by Roman forces.

ATARGATIS

Syrian Mermaid Goddess
Who Inspired a Slave Rebellion

PRONUNCIATION: a-TAR-ga-tiss

AKA: Derketo (Greek), Dea Syria or Deasura (Roman), Ataratheh or Tar'atheh (Aramaic)

APPEARANCE: Atargatis is often depicted as a goddess with long streaming hair and the lower body of a fish.

SYMBOLS:

• **Fish:** Atargatis's temple at Hierapolis was said to have a deep lake populated by sacred fish. The fish grew to an immense size, had names, and came when called. Some of the fish were adorned with gold, and stories say one had a jewel embedded in its fin.

• **Doves:** According to legend, a flock of doves nourished and raised the baby who Atargatis abandoned in the desert. She grew up to be the Assyrian queen Semiramis.

• **Lions:** Atargatis is sometimes depicted riding on a lion.

Overview

Atargatis is a mermaid goddess from ancient Syria. She is a goddess of the ocean, fertility, and love. According to the ancient Greek historian Herodotus, the legendary temple to Atargatis was located in Hierapolis, an ancient city in northern Syria. Inside, the walls and ceiling were gilded in gold, and so were the statues of Atargatis and her consort, Hadad.

The statue of Atargatis was encrusted in precious jewels, with a single glowing red gem in her forehead, bathing the temple in fiery light. No matter where you stood in the temple, the statue's eyes were said to follow you.

Her religion was a fierce and ecstatic one, led mostly by transgender women. It began in ancient Syria and was brought to ancient Italy by enslaved people from the region. Thus it became a religion of oppressed minorities in the Roman Empire.

Perhaps it's no surprise, then, that the religion of Atargatis fueled one of the largest slave revolts in Roman history. No, not Spartacus's rebellion—the First Servile War, which happened sixty years earlier. The leader of that rebellion—the Spartacus, you might say—was an enslaved man from Syria named Eunus. He was a fire-breather, miracle worker, and prophet of Atargatis.

What's Her Story?

There are a number of myths about Atargatis, most of which come to us from Roman writers. One of these myths, found in Diodorus Siculus's *Library of History*, is about how Atargatis came to be a mermaid. According to Diodorus, there was once a very deep lake in Syria, and Atargatis was worshipped on the shores of that lake.

The goddess Aphrodite cursed her to fall violently in love with one of her worshippers, a handsome young man. Atargatis slept with the man and bore him a daughter. But then, out of shame—and probably because the love spell wore off—she killed the young man and abandoned the baby girl in the desert. Then she threw herself into the lake.

When her body hit the water, it was changed into a fish's body. But her head remained human. Thus, the goddess Atargatis was portrayed as part woman, part fish.

Meanwhile, the baby was fed and protected by a flock of doves. Eventually, she was found and raised by the keeper of the king of Assyria's flocks, who named her Semiramis. Semiramis caught the eye of the king, and he married her. This is a mythological origin story for the historical queen Semiramis, who ruled ancient Assyria from 811–806 B.C.

Another myth connects Atargatis to the Seleucid Empire. According to this story, Queen Stratonice, wife of Seleucus I, dreamed that Atargatis had commanded her to build her a temple at Hierapolis. Seleucus I, who could deny his wife nothing, sent Stratonice to Hierapolis with an army of workers and architects and engineers—and asked his friend Combabus to oversee the whole thing.

Combabus was terrified of working closely with a woman. He was afraid that Stratonice might throw herself at him, he'd be powerless to resist, and then he would be in huge trouble with the king. So he castrated himself and put his severed genitals in a jeweled box—which he gave to the king for safekeeping.

Later, Combabus was accused of forcing himself on Stratonice. In a dramatic courtroom reveal, he asked the king to bring out the box in which he'd left his "greatest treasure." The king brought out the box and opened it to reveal Combabus's severed genitals nestled in a bed of herbs.

After this, Combabus moved into the temple, adopted women's dress, and became a priestess of Atargatis.

TRANSGENDER PRIESTESSES OF ATARGATIS

Atargatis's worshippers were usually assigned male at birth but underwent castration when inducted into her cult, then lived as women. While some of Atargatis's religious leaders may have been nonbinary or cisgender, many of them were probably people we would recognize today as transgender women. According to the satirical writer Lucian, those who wished to join Atargatis's religion castrated themselves during their induction, at the apex of a fierce and frenzied ritual of music and dance. Lucian was a satirist and probably sensationalized his account, but the religion of Atargatis wasn't the only one in the ancient world that involved castration. So it would not have been unheard of.

After the castration, the priestesses dressed and lived as women. They wore their hair long and wore makeup and silken robes, either saffron yellow or white with purple stripes. They were said to be astonishingly beautiful.

ATHENA

Greek Goddess of Wisdom, War, Statecraft, and the Heroic Endeavor

---

PRONUNCIATION: ah-THEE-na

AKA: Athene, Pallas, Pallas Athena, Minerva (Roman mythology),
Athena Parthenos ("Virgin"), Athena Promachos ("Who Fights in the Front Line"),
Athena Polias ("Protector of the City"), Athena Ergane ("the Industrious"),
Athena Hippia ("of the Horses" or "Equestrian")

APPEARANCE: She is often depicted as a beautiful and stately woman with blue-gray eyes and blond or black hair, wearing full battle regalia—including a gold helm, spear, and shield. Her aegis, or shield, was forged by the Cyclopes and has terrifying snakes along the edge and the famous head of the Gorgon Medusa in the center. She also wears a cape decorated with snakes.

SYMBOLS:

• Owls: These are her sacred bird and, in modern times,
have become symbols of wisdom because of their association with her.

• Olive trees: Athena gifted the people of ancient Athens an olive tree.
Olives, olive oil, and the wood from the trees became essential
to everyday life in ancient Greece.

Overview

Athena is the ancient Greek goddess of wisdom, war, strategy, crafts and artisans, and heroes. She is portrayed as a "virgin" goddess who does not have any male lovers. She is said to be Zeus's favorite child.

Athena is the daughter of Metis and Zeus, although some versions of the myths leave Metis out of the story. Metis was a Titaness and goddess of wisdom and counsel, and she helped Zeus work on his strategy to overthrow the Titans and Kronos. Zeus, being a serial predator, couldn't resist her beauty and intelligence.

When Metis became pregnant, Zeus heard a prophecy that she would bear a son greater than his father. And because the paranoid Zeus had learned nothing from his father, Kronos—who had also believed his child would overthrow him and devoured his own children to prevent this—Zeus decided to devour Metis whole to prevent his own usurping.

So the god who fought a war to overthrow his father because his father ate his children had now become the thing he'd rebelled against: a god who ate other gods because of a prophecy. Let's all pause to note the irony.

But Metis wasn't done with Zeus yet. She was still alive, somewhere inside Zeus's belly. She gestated Athena, and when the child grew up, she trained her in wisdom, cunning, and strategy (all from inside Zeus).

One day, Zeus had an epic migraine. It felt like his head was going to split in two. He called for Hephaestus, the blacksmith god, to come and help relieve the pain by cutting open his head—which is one way to treat a headache. Hephaestus did as Zeus asked—and out sprang Athena, fully grown, from Zeus's forehead, wearing her battle armor and ready to take her place among the Olympians.

Athena became one of the most popular of all the Olympian gods. She gave wise advice to gods and heroes and was a respected warrior goddess. She was slow to make war, but once she committed to battle, her strategy and cunning made all the other gods fear her. The goddess of victory, Nike, was part of Athena's retinue and walked the ancient battlefields with her.

Athena is a divisive goddess in modern times. While she is incredibly strong, resourceful, cunning, and revered, she also tended to treat women in mythology poorly. Athena is the goddess of the heroic endeavor—she was the patron of Odysseus, Cadmus, and Perseus, to name just a few heroes. In those myths, she appeared as a helper and guide to male heroes.

But her track record with women is much murkier. For example, she is the goddess who turned Medusa into a Gorgon and Arachne into a spider. While you can read these transformation stories as Athena giving these women power and agency by turning them into something "monstrous"—Medusa would never be a victim again, and Arachne would always be the world's best weaver—the stories also show us a darker side to Athena.

It's important to note that legends about Athena come down to us through the patriarchal lens. And that lens is committed to using Athena, a strong and "rational" goddess, as a tool of oppression for women and advancement for men. This might explain some of Athena's actions. It's also important to remember that the ancient Greeks saw their gods and goddesses as being very human—capable of petty jealousies, lusts, and wrath.

In modern times, you can find depictions of Athena in *Lore Olympus*, the Percy Jackson series, the *Blood of Zeus* TV series, *Clash of the Titans*, the *Hades* video game, and many other places.

What's Her Story?

One of the most famous myths about Athena involves the founding of Athens. Athena and Poseidon were competing over who would be the patron god of the up-and-coming city of Athens. Both wanted to receive the worship of the people living there. And in a fun twist, at this time in mythology, the people living in Athens were snake people—human from the waist up and snake from the waist down.

Athena and Poseidon each presented Kekrops, the king of the snake people, with a gift. The snake people were supposed to vote on these gifts, and whichever they liked better would determine which god they'd dedicate their city to.

Poseidon struck the ground and created a mighty saltwater spring. This would give the citizens access to the sea and open them up for trading. (In other myths, Poseidon created the first horse and gave it to the citizens.) Athena presented the citizens with the olive tree, which would give them food, shelter, and the ability to build mighty ships. The Athenians decided that Athena's gift was the greater one and named their city after her.

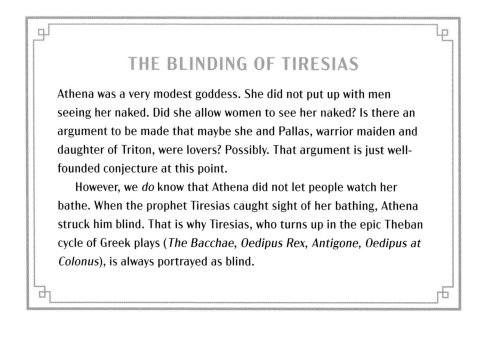

THE BLINDING OF TIRESIAS

Athena was a very modest goddess. She did not put up with men seeing her naked. Did she allow women to see her naked? Is there an argument to be made that maybe she and Pallas, warrior maiden and daughter of Triton, were lovers? Possibly. That argument is just well-founded conjecture at this point.

However, we *do* know that Athena did not let people watch her bathe. When the prophet Tiresias caught sight of her bathing, Athena struck him blind. That is why Tiresias, who turns up in the epic Theban cycle of Greek plays (*The Bacchae, Oedipus Rex, Antigone, Oedipus at Colonus*), is always portrayed as blind.

BAISHE NIANGNIANG

Thousand-Year-Old White Snake Goddess of China

PRONUNCIATION: BA-sha nyung-nyung

AKA: Madam White, White Lady, Bai Suzhen

APPEARANCE: Baishe Niangniang is often portrayed
as a young woman or a large white snake.

SYMBOLS:

• White snakes: Baishe Niangniang can transform into a white snake.

Overview

Baishe Niangniang is both a thousand-year-old white snake goddess and a young woman who braves great dangers for love. Her origin story begins in "The Legend of the White Snake," one of China's best-known folktales. She is also worshipped as a goddess in Chinese popular and traditional religion, bringing luck and good fortune to those who pray to her.

Her story has been retold many times in theater, TV, and film. It's a popular tale for stage musical, opera, and modern-dance adaptations, and versions of the story have been performed throughout China and worldwide. In 2010, Opera Boston produced an opera version by Chinese-American composer Zhou Long, entitled *Madame White Snake*. Zhou Long was awarded a 2011 Pulitzer Prize in Music for his work. More recently, the animated movies *White Snake* and *White Snake 2: The Tribulation of the Green Snake* are based on the story of Baishe Niangniang.

What's Her Story?

It all began with a white snake spirit who lived in a lake. One day, she consumed some immortality pills and immediately gained immense magical powers. She transformed into a young woman named Bai Suzhen and met Xu Xian, the young man who vomited the pills into the lake in the first place.

Naturally, they fell in love, got married, and opened a homeopathic pharmacy together.

But that's not the end of this story. A Buddhist monk named Fahai learned of Bai Suzhen's true identity and became determined to break them up. He tricked Bai Suzhen into revealing her snake form during a festival, and Xu Xian fell down dead from terror at seeing his wife's true form.

Bai Suzhen refused to let her husband stay dead. She embarked on a dangerous quest to steal a rare magical herb that could restore life, accompanied by her friend—Xiaoqing, a green snake who had also transformed into a woman.

After many trials and adventures, she and her friend found the herb, returned home, and restored Xu Xian to life, whereupon he swore his undying love for Bai Suzhen—white snake form and all. He didn't care that his wife was really a giant snake; he loved her just as she was.

But Fahai was not at all deterred in his quest to meddle in the couple's life. He kidnapped Xu Xian and imprisoned him in a temple. Bai Suzhen pursued them and fought a fearsome battle with Fahai. She used her powers to raise the waters in a nearby lake, but she realized that she could not defeat Fahai without drowning innocent bystanders—so she hesitated.

Fahai took advantage of her hesitation, capturing Bai Suzhen and imprisoning her under the Leifeng Pagoda. He declared that she would never be released until the palm tree in front of the pagoda burst into bloom. Unluckily for her, it wasn't a variety that bloomed very often, if at all. Bai Suzhen stayed in confinement for two decades.

Life went on. Her son with Xu Xian grew up to be a renowned scholar and earned top ranks in the imperial civil service exam. His scores were so high that the emperor gave him a hat decorated with flowers as a gift. The son returned home to great celebrations and visited the pagoda where his mother (unbeknownst to him) was imprisoned.

He happened to hang his flowered hat on a branch of the palm tree, which was enough to break the spell and free Bai Suzhen. She was reunited with Xu Xian and her son, and they lived out their lives happily.

The first known written version of this story appeared in a collection of tales called *Stories to Caution the World*, written in the seventeenth century. In the first extant version of the story, the Buddhist monk Fahai was the protagonist, heroically trying to rescue Xu Xian from the snake demoness who happened to be his wife. This version of the story is generally believed to be a cautionary tale about good and evil, with evil personified in the form of the snake woman. It ends with Bai Suzhen—there simply referred to as "Madam White"—imprisoned under the pagoda and Xu Xian renouncing sexual desire and retreating from the world.

Over the course of the next century and a half, the story evolved from a moralistic horror story to a love story, with Fahai cast as the antagonist. Bai Suzhen was very long-lived, and over the centuries, her powers grew until she became a goddess. Baishe Niangniang is the name she took in her more powerful goddess form.

SNAKE PEOPLE IN CHINESE MYTHOLOGY AND RELIGION

Baishe Niangniang is perhaps the most famous figure in Chinese mythology and religion who is both snake and human, but she's not the only one. Often, the snakes depicted in legend are not realistic, but fantastical beings that are part human or able to transform into a human. Others include Fuxi and Nüwa, twin siblings who in some legends were said to be the first humans—as well as creation gods in their own right, who created other humans out of clay. They are sometimes depicted as snakes with human heads.

Another is Gonggong, a Chinese water deity who is also described as having a human head (and sometimes human torso) with the body of a snake. Gonggong has destructive powers and is often blamed for bringing about chaotic and catastrophic events.

CORN MOTHER

First Woman of the Abenaki and Penobscot Creation Stories

AKA: Corn Maiden, First Mother

APPEARANCE: Corn Mother is sometimes depicted as an old woman and other times a young woman. Some artwork shows Corn Mother as having hair plaited into wheat ears.

SYMBOLS:

• Corn: Every part of corn is a symbol for Corn Mother—the kernels, the stalks, the silken hairs, the husks, and, of course, the corn itself.

Overview

Corn Mother appears in the mythologies and religions of many different Native American peoples, particularly those with a strong agricultural tradition. There are many different stories about how she saved her people.

In one series of stories, Corn Mother's people are facing imminent starvation. Corn Mother knows that she can help her people—by harvesting corn from her own body. How she does this isn't always clear; sometimes she produces corn by rubbing the kernels off her skin. Her people eat the lifesaving corn and are spared from starvation. But when they find out how she produced it, they are disgusted.

In some myths, they kill Corn Mother—either as punishment or as a sacrifice. Corn Mother gives very specific instructions on how she wants to be killed and where she wants to be buried so that her death will allow her people to have an everlasting field of corn.

Another version involves Corn Mother marrying a young man whose people are suffering from starvation. Again, she saves the people from starving by rubbing corn kernels off her flesh. When her husband discovers how she produces corn, he is disgusted, and Corn Mother flees. But when he follows her, she gives him corn kernels and explains how to cultivate them so that he is able to grow his own corn.

What's Her Story?

Perhaps one of the best-known versions of the Corn Mother story comes from the Penobscot people. In this story, Corn Mother plays a part in the creation myth. At the beginning of creation, Kloskurbeh, the All-Maker, worked with his nephew—a young man made from sea-foam—to create all life on earth.

The two men worked alone for a long time—until one day, a young woman appeared, born from the earth, sunlight, and dew. Because sunlight gives warmth and life, she was also a life-giver and nourisher of living things, and both men and animals loved her.

Kloskurbeh's nephew fell in love with the woman. They married and had many children, and the woman became known as First Mother and her husband as Great Nephew. Kloskurbeh taught their children how to live and hunt and survive, and then he went away to live in the north where he would remain until such time as he was needed.

Generations passed. The descendants of First Mother and Great Nephew became so numerous that they depleted the land—leading to widespread starvation. This caused First Mother immense grief. Children came to her and begged her for food, but she had none to give. She wept for her people, and for what she knew she must do.

Great Nephew was distraught. He wanted to help ease her sorrow, and he begged her to tell him how. To his horror, First Mother told him that the only way to ease her sadness was to kill her.

Great Nephew refused. He said that there must be some other way. Finally, he went to find Kloskurbeh and ask for his help. After a long journey to the ends of the earth, Great Nephew found his uncle and explained the situation. Surely, he pleaded, there must be some other way to ease First Mother's sorrow.

But Kloskurbeh agreed with First Mother. He told his nephew that in order to stop First Mother's weeping, he had to honor her wishes and kill her.

Great Nephew returned to his wife with a heavy heart, and First Mother explained to her husband exactly how she was to be killed. She instructed her husband to do the deed at noon, and then their sons were to take her by the hair and drag her body over the earth until the flesh was torn from her bones. Then they must bury her bones in the middle of the field and wait seven moons before returning to the spot where she was buried.

Her husband and sons did exactly as she asked. They said prayers over First Mother's body and the field where she was buried, and then they departed for seven moons.

When they returned, the field was covered in tall green plants, growing ears of corn. The corn was First Mother's flesh, given so her people would live. Corn became a staple of their diet, nourishing them, giving them strength and love.

The people were instructed not to eat all the corn, but to save some kernels to plant and continue the cycle every seven moons. And in this way, First Mother's gift is renewed forever.

CORN MAIDENS OF THE ZUNI PEOPLE

The Zuni of New Mexico have a fascinating story about Corn Maidens. Corn Maidens are women in Zuni religion and mythology who personify different strains of corn and the directions. The Blue Corn Maiden symbolizes the west; the White Corn Maiden is the east; the Speckled Corn Maiden stands for the zenith; while the Black Corn Maiden is the nadir—up and down, respectively. The Red Corn Maiden represents the south and the Yellow Corn Maiden the north.

According to some stories, the Corn Maidens made corn kernels by rubbing them off their own skin, much like we see in other versions. In some tellings, the Corn Maidens were offended by the suggestive movements of male dancers and flute players and fled to a land where it was always summer. The Corn Maidens return to dance when the corn is approximately knee-high. This story can be said to represent corn's agricultural cycle. In Zuni mythology and religion, the Corn Maidens have their own dance, the Zuni Molawai. It tells the story of their cyclical flight and return.

FREYJA

Golden Girl of the Viking Pantheon

———◆———

PRONUNCIATION: FRAY-a

AKA: Freya, Freja, Freia, Frua; the name means "Lady" in Old Norse
and may have been a title or honorific rather than a name;
it is related to the German word *frau* ("woman")

APPEARANCE: Freyja is usually depicted as a beautiful golden-haired woman. She
possesses a stunning necklace, or torc, called "Brísingamen" and a cloak made of
falcon feathers that bestows the power of flight on the wearer.

SYMBOLS:

• Cats: Freyja was said to travel in a sparkling chariot pulled by two black cats.

• Swine: Freyja was often accompanied by her familiar,
a boar named Hildisvíni, meaning "Battle Swine."

———◆———

Overview

Freyja is the Norse goddess of love, beauty, gold, and fertility. She loves jewelry, luxuries, and carnal pleasures. Her brother is Frey, a fertility god who rides on a golden boar. She was also the patron goddess of the *völva*—real-life

Norse sorceresses who practiced a type of magic called *seiðr*. According to Norse sagas, it was Freyja who taught *seiðr* to the rest of the gods.

Freyja is depicted as one of the calmer and more levelheaded Norse deities, but she has a bloodthirsty side. As a war goddess, she fought fiercely on the side of the Vanir—one of two competing pantheons of gods in Norse mythology—during the Aesir-Vanir war.

She also ruled over Fólkvangr, a meadow-like realm in the Norse afterlife. According to legend, half of all warriors killed in battle went there after death.

Freyja has been featured in many works of art in more modern times. The character Freia in Wagner's *Ring* cycle is based on Freyja. She was a popular subject for painters and artists in the late nineteenth and early twentieth centuries—and more recently in movies, TV series, novels, manga, and video games such as *God of War* and *SMITE*.

What's Her Story?

One myth about Freyja can be found in the *Poetic Edda* from the thirteenth century. There was once a young man named Ottar who had been orphaned early in life. He was a simple man: wise, generous, and honest. He was also a devoted worshipper of Freyja, and Freyja was very fond of him.

One day, another man came to Ottar's thingstead—the governing assembly in his village—and challenged Ottar's claim to his land. Ottar had to prove that his home belonged to him, and the only way to do that was by proving his ancestry. But since Ottar was adopted, he had no idea who his ancestors were.

Ottar returned home from the thingstead humiliated and terrified that he would lose everything he owned. But when he opened his front door, he got the surprise of his life—because the goddess Freyja was sitting at his kitchen table, waiting for him.

She invited him to come with her to Asgard, the realm of the Norse gods, to sort all this out. Ottar said yes—because who can say no to Freyja?—and in the next instant she transformed him into a boar for the journey.

On their way, they passed the home of a renowned *völva*, or sorceress. Freyja stopped and demanded the sorceress come out and recite Ottar's ancestry. This was a very powerful *völva* who was not used to being pushed around, but Freyja was a goddess—and nobody said no to her. So the *völva* did as she was told.

She recited Ottar's lineage back many generations, and it turned out Ottar was related to kings, queens, and even gods. In fact, his many-times-great-grandfather was Freyja's brother Frey. No wonder Freyja liked him so much.

Freyja then ordered the sorceress to offer Ottar memory beer so that he would remember the names of his ancestors. The sorceress did as asked, but as she offered the beer to Ottar, she whispered that it was laced with poison. Ottar was alarmed—but Freyja only laughed and bade Ottar to drink, for nothing bad could happen to him while he was under her protection.

Ottar went on to spend a very memorable day in Asgard with the gods, then returned home and got to keep his land. He lived a long, happy life and joined Freyja's entourage after death, as the boar Hildisvíni.

This story demonstrates Freyja's kindness—she would go to great lengths to help those she favored. Another story demonstrates Freyja's love of shiny things, and also highlights her promiscuity (she was a fertility goddess, after all). It's the tale of how she got her beautiful torc, Brísingamen.

In this story, Freyja is described as a concubine of Odin, the All-father—who was completely infatuated with her. But Odin was clingy, and Freyja needed space. So one day she snuck off to get some much-needed personal time and came upon four dwarves at a forge, crafting the most beautiful necklace she'd ever seen.

Freyja wanted that necklace. She offered gold and silver for it. But the dwarves refused to sell it. They told her that the only way they would give her the necklace was if she would have sex with each of them. Freyja agreed to these terms. She spent one night with each of the dwarves, and in return, she got her necklace.

And Odin may never have found out—except that Loki, the trickster god, was spying on Freyja the whole time. Knowing full well how obsessed

Odin was with her, he ran back to Odin to tattle. Furious, Odin ordered Loki to steal that necklace.

Loki transformed into a fly and snuck into Freyja's bedroom while she was sleeping. Freyja woke in the morning to find her precious necklace gone and immediately knew what had happened. She went straight to Odin to demand its return.

Odin told her that yes, he did have her necklace—and he would only return it if she cursed two powerful kings in Midgard to battle each other until a true Christian came to kill them. Freyja did as she was told and got her necklace back.

Meanwhile, somewhere in Midgard, two kings fell to fighting for more than a century, repeatedly rising again on the battlefield every time they died, before a Christian came along to put them out of their misery. It was a weird flex.

This tale was written by Christian priests around the fourteenth century. Some have argued that it's meant to cast Freyja's sexuality in a negative light and to impose Christian values about sex and promiscuity on the Norse pagan culture.

ANCIENT NORSE SORCERESSES

Freyja was the ruling goddess of the *völva*, ancient Norse sorceresses—and she was considered the most powerful of the *völva* herself. The *völva* were a real part of ancient pre-Christian Norse communities. They were female magic workers who traveled from village to village, plying their trade in exchange for food, a place to sleep, and other payment. The *völva* practiced *seiðr*, which involved prophesying the future.

HINE-NUI-TE-PŌ

Māori Goddess of Death and Protectress of the Dead

PRONUNCIATION: HEEN-eh ne-WEE te PO

AKA: Hine-tītama ("the Dawn Maid"), Great Woman of Night

APPEARANCE: Hine-nui-te-pō is sometimes depicted as a giant goddess who waits at the edge of the horizon to capture the souls of the dead. She has eyes made of greenstone, long wavy hair of kelp, a mouth like a barracuda, and a vagina lined with obsidian knives.

SYMBOLS:
• **The sunset:** Some traditions say that the red of the sunset derives from her.

Overview

Hine-nui-te-pō is the goddess of night and the dead in the Māori religious tradition of Aotearoa (the name for New Zealand in te reo Māori, the Māori language). She receives souls when they pass into the underworld. Some traditions state that she lurks on the horizon and that the red of the sunset is the glow of her fearsome vagina.

But Hine-nui-te-pō is not all frightening. In some traditions, she begins her story as Hine-tītama, the young and beautiful goddess of the dawn. She's also depicted as a protector goddess, shielding the newly dead souls from the menacing Whiro-te-tipua—the embodiment of evil in the Māori pantheon.

In pop culture, the character Te Fiti/Te Kā in Disney's *Moana* is very loosely based on Hine-nui-te-pō. She also appears in Karen Healey's YA fantasy novel *Guardian of the Dead*.

What's Her Story?

Hine-nui-te-pō began her life as Hine-tītama, the Dawn Maid. She was the daughter of Hineahuone, or Earth-Formed Woman, the first woman in the Māori religious tradition. When she was old enough, she married Tāne—god of light and of forests and birds. The two were happy, and they had many children.

But Hine-tītama didn't know her husband as well as she thought she did. One day, she set out to discover who her father was and uncovered a terrible secret: Her beloved husband, Tāne, was also her father. Stricken, Hine-tītama fled to the realm of the dead.

Tāne followed her, pleading with her to come back to him and their children. Hine-tītama refused, saying that she would see their children when they died and entered the underworld, and she would welcome and protect them when they did. Thus Hine-tītama, the Dawn Maid, became Hine-nui-te-pō, goddess of the night and the dead who welcomes the souls of the newly dead into the underworld.

Hine-nui-te-pō is sometimes described as a terrifying goddess who drags people down into death—but she is also seen as a benevolent force. In this depiction, she welcomes the souls of the dead and protects them from Whiro-te-tipua, another god who inhabits the underworld. In some versions of his story, he devours the souls of the recently dead, becoming stronger with each one—unless Hine-nui-te-pō stops him.

This is an especially urgent mission because if Whiro-te-tipua devours enough souls, he will gain the strength to break through the underworld and into the living world. Once there, he will devour every living thing he encounters. So by preventing Whiro-te-tipua from devouring souls, Hine-nui-te-pō is holding back an apocalypse.

Another story about Hine-nui-te-pō involves the Polynesian trickster hero Māui. While tales of Māui vary from culture to culture, he is often described as mischievous, clever, and generally well intentioned. One day, Māui got the idea that he could end death itself, thus rendering humankind immortal. All he had to do was enter Hine-nui-te-pō's body through her vagina, travel through her body, and emerge from her mouth—thus reversing the path of birth.

Māui came upon Hine-nui-te-pō asleep in the forest and decided to attempt it. He bade his companions, the local birds, to keep quiet while he attempted this feat so the goddess would not wake up. But when Māui attempted to enter the gigantic body of the goddess, he looked so ridiculous that the tiny *tīwaiwaka*—the New Zealand fantail—could not hold in its laughter. It burst into a loud, trilling laugh, which immediately woke the goddess. Hine-nui-te-pō woke and realized she was being violated. She immediately snapped shut her obsidian-lined vagina, cutting Māui in half.

THE HOMELAND OF THE MĀORI

Versions of tales about the trickster Māui appear in many Polynesian folktales and religious traditions, varying not just from island to island but also among different Māori communities on Aotearoa. According to Māori tradition, these stories and others originate from their ancestral homeland of Hawaiki. Māori legends speak of a deliberate, planned journey from an original ancient homeland in seven *waka hourua*, ocean-going, double-hulled canoes. From the earliest times to today, many Māori *iwi* (interrelated, family-based communities) can trace their *whakapapa*, or ancestry, back to one of the seven original *waka hourua*.

HUITACA

Muisca Goddess of Sex,
Drunkenness, and a Really Good Time

———◆◆———

PRONUNCIATION: WEE-ta-ka

AKA: Huitaca-Chibch, Xubchasgagua, Chía, Bachué

APPEARANCE: A beautiful Indigenous Colombian woman filled with joy,
laughter, warmth, sexual agency, and drunkenness.

SYMBOLS:

• White owls: Huitaca is turned into a white owl.

• The moon: Huitaca is associated with the moon because,
in some versions of her story, she is transformed into the moon
as punishment for refusing to go along with the patriarchy.

———◆◆———

Overview

Huitaca is a goddess of pleasure, sexual agency, drunkenness, song and
dance, the arts, witchcraft, the moon, water, and defying the patriarchy—all
the best things in life. She is also a goddess of rebellion in the religion of the
Muisca people of Colombia. The Muisca were one of the most advanced

civilizations in pre-Columbian South America. Their ancestral home was in the region of the Altiplano Cundiboyacense in the Colombian Andes.

Huitaca is one of the Muisca's most fascinating goddesses because of her spirit of rebellion. She dared to stand up to the patriarchy, and she paid the price. While you don't see Huitaca represented very often in popular culture, this goddess was a rebel and free spirit who deserves to have her tale told more often.

What's Her Story?

Whenever Huitaca showed up, a good time was sure to follow. She was the walking embodiment of joy, freedom, fertility, drunkenness, and sexuality—and that alone made her beautiful. But she wasn't just stunningly beautiful; she was also a rebel. Huitaca was extremely independent and didn't like being told what to do. She didn't care about anyone's arbitrary rules or laws. She had a quick temper, and she could be mercurial—especially when she'd been drinking (which was most of the time).

But for the most part, she was a fun goddess, one who always knew how to get the party started. And she loved throwing parties. As the goddess of drunkenness, witchcraft, singing and dancing, and sexuality, she had the power to turn any gathering into an absolute rager—with maybe an orgy happening in the back room.

Of course, invitations to those parties were in high demand. But not everyone loved them. Specifically, Bochica was not a fan.

Bochica was pretty much the embodiment of the patriarchy in the Muisca pantheon. He was described as a bearded man who came from the east—the Muisca equivalent to the Aztec god Quetzalcóatl. The mythology held that he taught his people an ethical and moral code, as well as metalworking, agriculture, and other skills.

Bochica was all about order and rigid rules, and he disapproved of everything about Huitaca. He did not think that drunken parties or sexual agency were appropriate for a goddess. But Huitaca laughed off his criticism and continued doing exactly what she wanted, refusing to conform to his demands.

Because she had the audacity not to obey him, Bochica cursed Huitaca. He turned her into a white owl, with eyes that could only see at night. Since owls are nocturnal, she became a creature of the night.

Bochica might have seen this as a bad thing. But Huitaca knew that all the best parties happened at night. Her domain became the night, and while her form might have changed, her true nature did not. She was still the goddess of a good time—so the joke was on Bochica, because it's unlikely that Huitaca gave up on throwing her parties. She probably just scratched him off the invite list.

Huitaca was all about women having agency and sexual freedom. Her defiance of the patriarchy makes a lot of sense when you consider the relatively egalitarian nature of Muisca society.

WOMEN IN MUISCA CULTURE
AND THE CODE OF NEMEQUENE

Women in ancient Muisca culture had a lot more agency and freedom than those in some of the other cultures discussed in this book. That's why an independent goddess like Huitaca was so important to them. Many of the most powerful deities in the Muisca pantheon were goddesses. This reflects the fact that prior to European colonization, the Muisca had a system of governance in which women had a certain amount of power and freedom, relatively speaking. The society was also matrilineal. While men were typically the rulers in their society, they usually derived their right to rule from their women relatives.

In Muisca society, men were primarily hunter-gatherers, while women handled agriculture, child-rearing, textile making, and ceramic making. They were also in charge of governance—making major decisions and codifying rules for their people. The code of law in Muisca society was called the Code of Nemequene. Both wives and husbands were harshly punished for infidelity, and it was forbidden for a man to leave his wife. Incest and rape were also punished severely, and if a woman died in labor, her spouse had to pay her family a fine.

ISHTAR

Bearded Goddess of
War and Sex in Ancient Mesopotamia

PRONUNCIATION: ISH-tar

AKA: Inanna (ancient Sumerian), Astarte (Phoenician)

APPEARANCE: Ishtar is sometimes represented as a young cisgender woman and sometimes as gender nonconforming, including with a beard. As a war goddess, she wears wings and bears weapons.

SYMBOLS:

• **Lions:** Lions were potent symbols of power and rulership in ancient Mesopotamian cultures.

• **Doves:** Figurines of doves were found in temples of Ishtar (or her precursor, Inanna) dating back to as early as the 3000s B.C. The Greek word for "dove" may have been derived from "bird of Ishtar" in Semitic.

• **The planet Venus:** In keeping with Ishtar's gender nonconformity, she is associated with Venus, the planet sometimes seen as feminine in the morning and masculine at night. The planet Venus was often represented by an eight- or sixteen-pointed star in Ishtar's iconography.

• **The door of a storehouse:** This indicates her status as a goddess of agricultural fertility.

Overview

With a history of worship going back to 4000 B.C., Ishtar is one of the most ancient goddesses known to history. She appeared in ancient Mesopotamia as a goddess of war, fertility, and sex, and was worshipped by ancient cultures such as the Assyrians, Akkadians, Sumerians, and Babylonians.

Ishtar had a capricious nature. She was often represented in ancient texts as hotheaded and reckless, with a lust for conquest.

Ishtar was sometimes depicted as a cisgender woman but other times as nonbinary or gender nonconforming. According to one hymn, she was "bearded with a beard, [and] clothed in splendor." Some believe she could be an early representation of a transgender woman or intersex person. Ishtar's gender nonconforming nature may have been rooted in her association with Venus (the planet, not the goddess). In ancient Mesopotamian religions, Venus was sometimes seen as having two genders: feminine in the morning, masculine at night.

Ishtar has influenced and appeared in a number of modern works of art, including movies, manga, paintings and art installations, TV shows, and opera. A 1987 comedy film called *Ishtar* has a character based on her (it famously bombed). Sailor Venus from the manga series *Sailor Moon* is loosely based on Ishtar. Ishtar, and characters influenced by her, appear in TV shows such as *Hercules: The Legendary Journeys* and *Buffy the Vampire Slayer*. A 2003 opera by John Craton, *Inanna: An Opera of Ancient Sumer*, depicts her life and adventures.

What's Her Story?

Perhaps the most well-known story about Ishtar is recorded in the *Epic of Gilgamesh*. This is one of the earliest surviving works of literature still in existence; it dates to around 2100 B.C. In the epic, Gilgamesh and his friend Enkidu killed Humbaba, the fearsome guardian of the Cedar Forest. Gilgamesh's warrior skills caught the eye of the goddess Ishtar.

Of course, Ishtar was a goddess of sex and fertility. Not only was she drop-dead gorgeous, but she knew exactly what she wanted—and she fully expected to get it. So she walked right up to Gilgamesh and told him what she wanted. She wanted him, in her bed, right now. Gilgamesh turned her down in a very insulting speech, in which he pointed out that Ishtar didn't exactly have a history of treating her lovers well. (Plus it was extremely obvious that he and Enkidu were *an item*, so she didn't have much of a chance to begin with.)

Incensed by his insults, Ishtar unleashed the Bull of Heaven on Gilgamesh—but he and Enkidu killed the beast. In punishment, the gods determined that Enkidu must die, sending the grief-stricken Gilgamesh on a quest for immortality.

In his speech criticizing Ishtar's treatment of her other partners, Gilgamesh referenced another famous story—Ishtar's descent into the underworld and her treatment of her husband Tammuz, a handsome young shepherd, fertility god, and total himbo (who kind of deserved it). In this story, Ishtar decided to conquer the underworld, which was ruled by her sister Ereshkigal. She rolled up to the massive gates and boldly demanded to be let in—or else she'd smash the gate and unleash the dead into the world above to devour the living.

Ereshkigal coolly bade her gatekeeper to let Ishtar in. The seven gates of the underworld swung open, and Ishtar passed through each of them, but at each gate, she lost a talisman of her power. Her crown, her jewelry, her girdle, her raiment were all shed—until finally Ishtar stood before Ereshkigal naked and powerless. Ereshkigal struck her dead with a word.

Meanwhile, up in the world of the living, everything fell into chaos. People and animals lost their sex drive, and reproduction halted. Ishtar was the goddess of fertility, after all, and without her, there could be no sex or childbearing.

In alarm, the god Ea created two messengers from the dirt beneath his nails—the *kurgarra* and *assinnu*—to revive Ishtar from death and bring her back to the world of the living. The *kurgarra* and *assinnu* were gender nonconforming, said to be neither man nor woman. They healed Ishtar and then fled with her from the underworld, pursued by a host of demons. In Ishtar's trip back to the living world, she encountered people from her life—her vizier, her beautician, her son—and seeing how deeply they mourned her, she stopped the demons from dragging them off to the underworld in her stead.

Finally, Ishtar encountered her husband Tammuz. Instead of mourning his wife, he was lounging on her throne, enjoying all the luxuries of her position while cavorting with beautiful women. Enraged, Ishtar bade the demons to drag him to the underworld in her place.

Later, however, Ishtar realized she missed Tammuz. He might have had his flaws, but he was a really good time. So she decreed that he may live with her half the time and with Ereshkigal in the underworld the other half. (She didn't want to ruin her sister's fun either.)

This story resembles that of Persephone and Hades in Greek mythology. Like that story, this myth about Ishtar and Tammuz is considered an early fertility myth, told to explain the seasonal cycles. Such stories may have their roots in the dawn of agriculture in ancient Mesopotamia.

WAR-DANCING
TRANSGENDER PRIESTESSES

Ishtar was said to have the power to change women into men and men into women. During her festivals, men dressed in women's clothes on their left side, and women dressed as men on their right side. And as with the Syrian fertility goddess Atargatis, Ishtar was believed to have had transgender priestesses.

Like her loyal retainers and rescuers in her myth, Ishtar's priestesses were also known as the *kurgarra* and *assinnu*. In the Babylonian poem the *Epic of Erra*, they are described as women "whose maleness Ishtar turned female, for the awe of the people." In the myth, the *assinnu* revived Ishtar from death using a magical plant given to them by the god Ea. The *assinnu* in Ishtar's temples were also known as healers. As for the *kurgarra*, they were often depicted with weapons and were said to perform war dances—while wielding swords, knives, and clubs—in Ishtar's temples as part of their worship.

ISIS

PRONUNCIATION: EYE-siss

AKA: Aset, Eset, Auset

APPEARANCE: Isis often appears wearing a red sheath dress and a headdress that looks like a throne. In later iconography, she is shown wearing a headdress of a cow's horns with a sun disk between them. Sometimes she is depicted in a kneeling posture with wings spread.

SYMBOLS:

- **Animals:** Isis has associations with various animals, including cows, scorpions, sows, and birds.
- **Thrones:** Isis wears a throne headdress and is a goddess of kingship.

Overview

Stories of Isis first appear on the walls of pyramids of the Fifth Dynasty of Egypt, dating from around the 2400s B.C. These texts—called the Pyramid Texts—are composed of spells written to aid the royal dead in the afterlife.

67

Isis is associated with healing and magic. She was an ideal wife and mother and a goddess of motherhood and fertility. She was also associated with life, death, and rebirth, and played an important role in ancient Egyptian beliefs about the afterlife. As a goddess of healing, Isis's name figured prominently in healing spells from ancient Egypt.

Isis's role evolved over time, and she was eventually adopted as an important goddess in Greece and Rome. The name we know her by today, Isis, is what the Greeks called her. Her original Egyptian names—Aset, Eset, or Auset—were related to the Egyptian word for "throne."

Isis's symbolism and significance have long outlived her reign as an ancient Egyptian deity. In modern Egypt during the 1920s and 1930s, Isis figured prominently as a national symbol of the movement for independence from British rule. Over the years, she has been featured often in pop culture. Examples include TV shows such as *The Secrets of Isis* and *Supernatural*, the 2016 film *Gods of Egypt*, romance author Nina Bangs's Castle of Dark Dreams series, and video games such as *Age of Mythology*.

What's Her Story?

Perhaps the most important myth about Isis involves the resurrection of her brother-husband, Osiris. There were many different versions written on the walls of pyramids and on the insides of coffins for thousands of years, starting as early as the 2400s B.C. It's likely that the most ancient written versions represent a much older oral tradition.

Her story begins with the god Osiris ruling Egypt. He was the son of Geb, god of the earth, and Nut, goddess of the sky. Ruling alongside him were his sisters and wives, Isis and Nephthys.

Osiris had a brother, Set, who absolutely could not stand him. Some versions say Set hated Osiris because Osiris once kicked him. Others say it was because Osiris was sleeping with Nephthys, who Set felt was his consort. But Set was also a god of chaos and violence, so it might just have been his nature to stir up trouble.

One day, Set got fed up with Osiris strutting around Egypt acting all regal. So he murdered Osiris, cut up his corpse, scattered the pieces all over Egypt, and ascended the throne himself.

Everyone was upset over Osiris's death, but nobody more than Isis. She searched everywhere for her husband's body. Some legends connect the annual flooding of the Nile with her tears. Eventually, she found and assembled all the pieces of Osiris's body—with the help of other gods, such as Anubis, god of embalming. (Anubis's methods provided the mythic basis for the ancient Egyptian tradition of mummification.)

Once the body was reassembled, Isis spoke spells over Osiris's body in a great outpouring of emotion that was also part of the spell. She wept for her husband, she expressed deep and unending grief, she railed at him for leaving her, and she spoke of her unfulfilled sexual desire for him. All of these things were meant to exhort him to return to her, but none of them worked.

Finally, Isis transformed into a bird and fanned her wings, sending the breath of life into Osiris and restoring him enough to have sex with her and conceive her son Horus. (Some myths say she also did this as a bird.) Osiris then retired to the Duat, or underworld, to rule.

This myth explains Isis's religious role in the Egyptian afterlife—and demonstrates her magical prowess. But it's not the only myth in which Set tried to ruin Isis's life and harm her loved ones.

In another myth, Set tried to kill Isis and the infant Horus. Isis fled to the marshes with the baby, disguising herself as an old woman. In the marshes, many scorpions and other poisonous creatures tried to attack Horus; Isis had to protect him with spells. Finally, the goddess Serket, who ruled over venomous animals, sent seven giant scorpion bodyguards to protect them.

The marsh was not a comfortable place to sleep, even for a goddess. At night, Isis emerged with her baby and her seven giant scorpion bodyguards, looking for a place to sleep. She knocked on the door of a wealthy woman, but when the woman saw the disreputable-looking, disguised Isis and her seven giant scorpion bodyguards, she slammed her door in fear.

Isis then went to the door of a poor fisherwoman. The woman let Isis in, shared a humble meal with her, and offered her a bed. Isis gladly accepted.

Meanwhile, the seven giant scorpions were infuriated at the wealthy woman's treatment of Isis. Conspiring together, they all poured their poison into the biggest, most dangerous scorpion, Tefen, who snuck into the wealthy woman's home and stung her child.

The child's wails woke his mother, who ran out into the street for help. The commotion woke Isis, and she went outside. When the wealthy woman explained the situation, Isis knew exactly what had happened. She followed the woman back to her house and spoke spells over the child's body, calling on the poison to come out of the child and fall upon the ground.

The poison obeyed, and the child healed. As a parting gift, Isis gave the community spells for repelling poison—which they continued to use down through history.

ISIS IN THE DUAT

The Duat is the underworld of ancient Egyptian mythology, and Isis was said to have special influence there. Her name appears more than eighty times in the Pyramid Texts, and she figures prominently in the *Book of the Dead.* She was believed to be the mother of the four gods who protected the canopic jars that contained the organs of the deceased. Her image, with wings outstretched, was often painted on ancient Egyptian coffins.

Some believed that, just as she breathed life into Osiris, Isis could also restore life and breath to the newly dead in the afterlife. A set of funerary texts called the Books of Breathing were sometimes buried with the dead in the later Egyptian Empire and into the Roman period. They were styled as letters given by Isis to Osiris, instructing him on how to breathe in the afterlife. It was believed that these letters would impart the same breath to those they were buried with.

ĪTZPĀPĀLŌTL

Skeletal Warrior Goddess of the Aztecs

---◆---

PRONUNCIATION: eetz-pa-PA-lote

AKA: Obsidian Butterfly, Clawed Butterfly

APPEARANCE: Ītzpāpālōtl is sometimes depicted as a woman with long, flowing hair, brandishing a femur or severed leg, and other times as a skeletal warrior goddess with obsidian, knife-tipped wings.

SYMBOLS:

• **Moths:** Ītzpāpālōtl is associated with a particular moth: *Rothschildia orizaba*, or the Orizaba silkmoth.

• **Birds, bats, and butterflies:** In some pre-Columbian cultures, an Ītzpāpālōtl-like goddess is associated with bats, sometimes referred to as "black butterflies" in certain mythology.

• **Fire:** An affinity to fire occurs in some myths about Ītzpāpālōtl.

---◆---

Overview

Ītzpāpālōtl, also known as the Obsidian Butterfly, is a warrior goddess in Aztec mythology who appears as a skeletal figure with obsidian butterfly wings tipped with flint knives. She is beautiful, otherworldly, and deadly.

She rules over the mythical realm of Tamoanchan, the place where the current race of humans was created from the powdered bones and blood of human sacrifice victims stolen from Mictlan, the Aztec underworld. Tamoanchan is also the place where infants who die in childbirth are said to go. In this realm grows a tree with 400,000 nipples, where the infants can replenish their strength and prepare to be reborn.

Ītzpāpālōtl has both destroyer and protector qualities. She is one of the Tzitzimime, or Star Demons—fearsome goddesses who live in the sky and only descend to earth in absolute darkness. They are especially dangerous during solar eclipses. Ītzpāpālōtl is sometimes depicted as a frightening demon goddess who devours men, but she also protects midwives and women in childbirth.

Ītzpāpālōtl has inspired several recent characters in pop culture, such as Orizaba the moth fairy in the Disney Junior series *Elena of Avalor* and the monster in the Netflix horror movie *No One Gets Out Alive*. The Itzpapalotl Tessera, a land formation on the planet Venus, is named after her.

What's Her Story?

The stories we know about Ītzpāpālōtl from pre-Columbian times are fragmentary, mainly because of the colonization and genocide suffered by the Aztec people at the hands of Europeans. After the Aztec city of Tenochtitlán was destroyed by Hernán Cortés in 1521, the Aztecs and other central Mesoamerican cultures were colonized by Spain. Their populations were decimated by violence and disease, and the Spanish sought to assimilate those who survived.

Descendants of the Aztecs living under Spanish rule were kept from learning about their own culture or reading and writing in their native language, Nahuatl. However, some Aztecs and their descendants wrote down pre-Columbian mythology, history, cosmology, geography, herbal knowledge, religious practice, and more as an act of resistance and to preserve their cultural heritage.

This story comes from one such document—the *Codex Chimalpopoca*, a collection of post-conquest manuscripts written in Spanish and Nahuatl. It includes both the pre-conquest history of Indigenous people in central Mexico and a study of Aztec cosmology and religious beliefs. In this story, Ītzpāpālōtl and the goddess Chimalman (meaning "Shield-Hand") manifested on earth as two deer, each with two heads. Two Cloud Serpent brothers, Xiuhnel and Mimich, also came to earth as men in order to hunt. (Cloud Serpents, or *Centzonmīmixcōah* in Nahuatl, were deities of the northern stars. The Aztecs and other ancient Mesoamerican cultures sometimes described the Milky Way as a Cloud Serpent.)

Xiuhnel and Mimich spied the two-headed deer and pursued them for a night and a day. By sunset of the second night, they were exhausted. They built a hut for shelter, but no sooner had they taken their rest than two beautiful women came to the door. Now the hunters had become the hunted.

The women called to Xiuhnel and Mimich in compelling voices, pleading to be invited in. Xiuhnel, unable to resist the temptation, relented and invited one of the women inside. She entered, and she and Xiuhnel lay down together and had sex. Immediately afterward, the woman ripped open Xiuhnel's chest and devoured his heart. Mimich, looking on in horror, realized that the beautiful, bloodthirsty woman was none other than Ītzpāpālōtl, terrifying Star Demon and Obsidian Butterfly.

With one heart-devouring goddess eying him from across the room and the other's haunting calls drifting in from outside, Mimich quickly snatched up his fire-starting tool, lit a fire, and threw himself into it. Ītzpāpālōtl followed and pursued him through the fire for a night and a day.

Finally, at the end of his strength, Mimich hid inside a barrel cactus. Ītzpāpālōtl descended after him. It was there that Mimich felled her with a lucky shot.

The Fire Lords helped Mimich retrieve the body of Ītzpāpālōtl and set it on fire. Ablaze, her body transformed—first into blue flint, second into white flint, third into yellow flint, and fourth into black flint. Mimich took up the white flint, which held Ītzpāpālōtl's soul, and he was transformed into the god of the hunt, Mixcoatl.

In this myth, the tool Mimich used to start a fire was called a fire drill. Fire drills are composed of a wooden rod and a piece of wood with a slight cavity. The rod is rotated or rubbed very quickly against the cavity, creating friction that starts a fire. You can rotate it between two palms or use a bow-like tool with the string wrapped around the rod to make it rotate faster. It is deceptively simple but requires great skill to use effectively. Mimich's counterpart, the god Mixcoatl, was believed to be the one who brought the fire drill to the Aztec people.

Ītzpāpālōtl is also referred to as the "goddess of flint" in this myth. Flint was an important material to the Aztecs; they used it to make sacred knives, or *tecpatl*. These knives were extremely sharp and deadly, both as implements of sacrifice and as weapons of war.

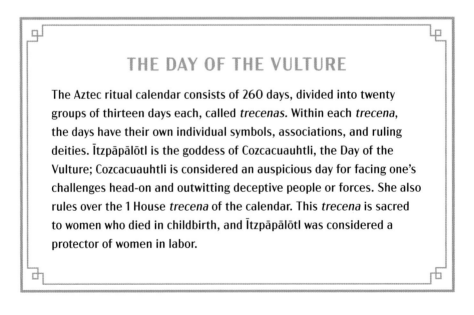

THE DAY OF THE VULTURE

The Aztec ritual calendar consists of 260 days, divided into twenty groups of thirteen days each, called *trecenas*. Within each *trecena*, the days have their own individual symbols, associations, and ruling deities. Ītzpāpālōtl is the goddess of Cozcacuauhtli, the Day of the Vulture; Cozcacuauhtli is considered an auspicious day for facing one's challenges head-on and outwitting deceptive people or forces. She also rules over the 1 House *trecena* of the calendar. This *trecena* is sacred to women who died in childbirth, and Ītzpāpālōtl was considered a protector of women in labor.

KALI

Hindu Goddess of Time, Death,
and the End of the World

PRONUNCIATION: KAH-lee

AKA: Mahakali, Dakshina Kālikā, Chaturbhuja Kali, Daksinakali

APPEARANCE: Kali has blue or black skin, wild disheveled hair, a lolling tongue and bloodstained mouth, and many arms—four or ten, depending on the incarnation. She is depicted mostly naked, wearing a garland of skulls around her neck and a skirt made of severed arms.

SYMBOLS:

• **A bloodstained sword:** This weapon represents knowledge of the divine.

• **A severed head:** The head represents the ego, which must die for a person to attain enlightenment and freedom from the cycle of death and rebirth.

• **A cup or bowl:** This is to catch the blood running from the severed head. Sometimes it's a *kapala*, or a vessel made out of a skull.

Overview

Kali is one of the most powerful goddesses in the Hindu pantheon. She is often interpreted as a bloodthirsty goddess of destruction, and her imagery

can be violent and fiercely sexual. She does possess those traits, but it's a mistake to interpret her as *only* destructive without looking beyond her fearsome iconography. If you look closer, you'll see that there is much more to Kali than that. With one of her free hands, she is often seen making the *abhayamudra*—a gesture of peace, protection, and reassurance.

Her destruction is often, at its heart, protective. In some of her legends, she is described as the embodiment of the pure, unbridled rage of other goddesses such as Parvati and Durga—a rage that arises from an urge to protect.

Kali is also seen as a maternal goddess and as a supreme goddess of reality, time, and the end of the world. Even her association with doomsday is not all negative; she heralds the death of creation so that a new world can be born.

What's Her Story?

Perhaps the best known story about Kali appears in the *Devi Mahatmyam*. The demon Raktabija ("Blood-Seed") was terrorizing all of creation. The gods tried to stop him, but every time a drop of his blood was spilled, another demon arose of identical strength and power as Raktabija. Thus, in trying to defeat this demon, the gods only created an army of Raktabijas.

So the gods combined their *shakti*, or divine powers, to create a being capable of defeating this fearsome demon. That's when Kali first strode onto the battlefield—an awe-inspiring vision of rage with a lolling tongue, blue-black skin, and many arms in which she held all the most potent weapons of the gods.

Kali wasted no time in engaging Raktabija and his minions in battle— and whenever she spilled blood, she drank every last drop so it would have no time to form another demon. Finally, she beheaded Raktabija with her sword, then drank the deluge of blood that gushed from his neck so that no more demons would rise. Only then was Raktabija truly defeated.

There are different versions of this story. In one, the warrior goddess Durga produced Kali—she emerged from Durga's forehead as a manifestation of her rage. In others, Kali was formed from the goddess Parvati.

In another version, Kali was unable to rein in her destructive side after defeating her demon enemies, and she began a bloody rampage of her own. None of the other gods could stop her until her consort, Shiva, stepped in and tried to talk her down. But Kali would not listen. Consumed by battle fury, she knocked Shiva down and danced upon his prone body. Only then did she realize what she was doing—and she stepped back as her battle rage dissolved into remorse.

The image of Kali dancing on Shiva's body has been interpreted many different ways. For example, Kali's triumph over Shiva may carry a message that the human mind can never entirely control the wild, natural world or humanity's natural instincts.

HISTORY OF KALI

Kali is an ancient goddess. The earliest mention of Kali as we know her today occurs in the *Devi Mahatmyam*, which dates from approximately the sixth century A.D. But precursors to her may have appeared as early as the *Rig Veda*, a collection of hymns written in Sanskrit that dates from approximately 1700–1000 B.C. In these writings, she is depicted as the black tongue of Agni, the god of fire. (He had seven tongues.) Raatri, goddess of the night, and the ogress Long Tongue—who devours religious offerings—may also be early aspects of Kali.

Another possible precursor to Kali is Kotravai, a Tamil war goddess who also rules over agriculture, fertility, and the hunt. She is one of the most ancient goddesses in Tamil tradition, first mentioned in poetry dating from as early as 300 B.C. Kotravai is known to be a warlike goddess who inspires her own worshippers to cut their heads and body parts in their devotion.

MAMI WATA

African and Afro-Caribbean
Mermaid Goddess and Snake Charmer

———◆◆———

PRONUNCIATION: MA-mee WA-ta

AKA: La Sirene, Lasirenn, Mamiwatra, Yemaya, Maman Dio, River Mama, Mmuommiri, Mamadjo, Mohana

APPEARANCE: Mami Wata is a beautiful dark-skinned mermaid.

SYMBOLS:

• **Snakes:** Mami Wata may also appear as either half snake, half woman or as a snake charmer with a large snake wound around her body.

• **Mirrors, watches, and jewelry:** She is often depicted with these and other expensive and shiny things.

———◆◆———

Overview

Mami Wata is a water goddess who plays an important role in the religious practices of communities throughout Africa, with a nexus in southeastern Nigeria. She is also prominent in African–diaspora communities in countries including Brazil, Cuba, Grenada, Jamaica, Trinidad and Tobago, and many others.

Like water itself, she is both beguiling and powerful, life-giving and dangerous. Mami Wata is often portrayed as a mermaid or half woman, half snake. Some traditional portrayals depict her as a snake charmer—a beautiful woman with a large snake wrapped around her body, its head winding up between her breasts.

In mythology, Mami Wata sometimes appears as a capricious spirit who "tests" those who encounter her, such as by kidnapping people to test their mettle or by leaving tempting belongings, such as her golden hand mirror and jewelry, to see who will steal them.

She is also sexually assertive and possessive, demanding fidelity of those she sleeps with. This part of her character may attest to an ancient connection to fertility goddesses in older African tradition. Mami Wata's partners are often men, but the Haitian version of her—Lasirenn—has a connection to queer Black women. Some depictions of her are genderqueer or gender-fluid, and she occasionally manifests as a cisgender man.

Mami Wata has also evolved into what some call a "capitalist" goddess, bringing great wealth and financial success to those she favors most.

Mami Wata has proved a compelling subject for artists across all genres, including novelists, poets, visual artists, musicians, and filmmakers. She appears in Ta-Nehisi Coates's novel *The Water Dancer*, on TV shows including *Lost Girl* and *River Monsters*, and in the novel *Lagoon* by Nigerian-American writer Nnedi Okorafor, among many other places.

What's Her Story?

Mami Wata is known for stalking rivers and shorelines, kidnapping sailors and swimmers in and around the water. She spirits them away to her underwater realm and keeps them there for a time to test their worthiness. Those she finds lacking, she takes as sacrifices. But those who pass her tests are returned to land, clothes completely dry, to find that their stations in life are much improved. Mami Wata will grant wealth, beauty, fame, and fortune to her chosen favorites.

In some legends, Mami Wata appears as a beautiful mermaid, combing her long, luxurious hair and gazing at herself in a mirror. When a person happens upon her, she flees the scene, leaving her mirror and other valuable items—such as watches and jewelry—behind.

If the interloper takes her belongings, Mami Wata will haunt their dreams, demanding they return what's hers. In exchange, she will offer sexual favors—but will also expect lifelong fidelity. Those who agree will be blessed with great wealth and good fortune; those who refuse will bring ruin upon themselves and their families.

Mami Wata's powers encompass both the positive and negative: fertility and death, wealth and financial ruin, health and illness. Like the water itself, she can both give life and livelihood and take them away.

As a fertility goddess, she may appear to her favorite followers as a sex worker or otherwise promiscuous woman. She will offer sex and then reveal herself as a goddess. She asks no less than complete sexual fidelity and sworn secrecy—with great financial reward for those who agree and calamity for those who refuse. In some traditions, women look to Mami Wata to cure infertility.

Mami Wata is sometimes blamed for illnesses, especially long, lingering illnesses that sap energy. She is both cause and cure; some traditions hold that such maladies are a sign of her disapproval, and only she can heal the sufferer.

Mami Wata is also said to have a particular affinity for women and children and to be a protector of women in abusive relationships and mothers parted from their children.

WORSHIP AS AN ACT OF RESISTANCE

Mami Wata may have evolved from beliefs about water spirits within diverse African communities. Her tradition grew and changed as she traveled across the sea along with people stolen from their homes and forced into slavery during the transatlantic slave trade. Worship of Mami Wata was recorded on plantations as early as the 1700s.

Europeans went to great lengths to suppress worship of Mami Wata and other non-Christian deities, introducing dire punishments for disobedience. Even so, many enslaved people continued to worship her in secret and at great risk as an act of resistance. Worship of Mami Wata also spread throughout enslaved populations in the Caribbean, as well as Central and South America, where it continues to this day.

THE MORRIGAN

Ancient Irish Goddess of War and Battle Frenzy

———◆◆———

PRONUNCIATION: the MOR-ri-gan

AKA: The Badb ("the Scald Crow"), Red-Haired Macha, Nemain ("Battle Frenzy"),
Fea the Deathly, Be Neit ("the Woman of Battle")

APPEARANCE: The Morrigan is a shape-shifter. You may meet her on the battlefield
as an old woman or a young maiden, or perhaps a crow, wolf, or cow. She is also
depicted as a triplicate goddess, appearing as three women instead of one.

SYMBOLS:

• Crows: The Morrigan can transform into a crow—her name in this form is
"the Badb." This symbol is fitting, as crows are carrion birds
(meaning they eat the flesh of dead animals) and must have been
common sightings in the aftermath of a battle.

• Cattle: The Morrigan is also associated with cattle and is sometimes interpreted
as a cow goddess. Cows in ancient Ireland were symbols of status and wealth, and
intertribal conflict often revolved around cattle raids.

———◆◆———

Overview

The Morrigan is a terrifying Irish Celtic goddess said to embody the chaos and horror of war. She shifts shapes, she predicts doom, and she inspires armies both to battle frenzy and overwhelming fear with her fierce war poetry.

The Morrigan also foretells death. In mythology, she is often depicted washing the clothes, chariot trappings, and armor of doomed heroes in a river. Some accounts are even more gruesome. In the *Triumphs of Turlough*, a pseudo-historical fourteenth-century account of Anglo-Normans invading the Irish territory of Thomond, the Morrigan is described as washing a pile of severed heads and other body parts in the river, covering the surface of the water with an oily scrim of gory brains and hair.

A general on his way to battle noticed this grisly scene and stopped to ask who this woman was and what she was doing. He realized with dawning horror that the body parts belonged to him and his *entire army* and that he was fated to lose the battle he was marching to.

This bloodthirsty, mighty goddess has inspired many operas, songs, plays, novels, epic poems, video games, and other works throughout the years, capturing imaginations with her untempered fury and terrifying power.

In modern times, you might catch sight of her in Sarah J. Maas's fantasy series A Court of Thorns and Roses; in video games such as *SMITE*, *Vampyr*, *Darkstalkers*, *Mount & Blade Warband: Viking Conquest*, and *Bloodforge*; and in Dianne K. Salerni's The Eighth Day series.

What's Her Story?

Perhaps the first recorded appearance of the Morrigan occurs in *Táin Bó Cúailnge*, or *The Cattle Raid of Cooley*—an epic tale sometimes described as the Irish *Iliad*. In the story, the Morrigan appeared to the hero Cuchulainn on the battlefield as a beautiful young maiden—offering him sex, favor, and help in battle. Cuchulainn did not recognize her and turned her down.

Enraged, the Morrigan swore to hinder him—threatening to be the eel that tripped him in the stream, the she-wolf that stampeded cows in his direction, the hornless red heifer who led the herd to trample him.

All of this came to pass in Cuchulainn's next battle. During the fight, Cuchulainn wounded the interfering animals—breaking the eel's ribs, bursting the she-wolf's eye, and breaking the heifer's leg. He won his battle, but only after suffering serious injuries.

After the battle, Cuchulainn encountered a woman milking a cow by the river—and she had wounds corresponding to those he had given the animals. Cuchulainn recognized the Morrigan and ritually healed her, saying he never would have hurt her if he had known who she was.

The Morrigan saw this as too little, too late.

Losing the favor of the Morrigan had serious repercussions for Cuchulainn, eventually leading to his death. On the road to his final battle, he encountered the Morrigan washing his armor in the river—an omen that he would soon die violently.

He came upon her again on the side of the road in triplicate—as three old women who shamed him into breaking a personal prohibition, or *geas*, against eating dog meat. Eating the dog meat weakened him enough for his enemies to kill him.

That's one story about what happened to a hero who turned down the Morrigan on the battlefield. But the Morrigan offered her favor to another mythical warrior in a second tale, and this time, he said yes.

The one who accepted is the Dagda, a powerful god and Druid-like figure in Irish mythology. The Dagda came across the Morrigan on the eve of an important battle, straddling a river and washing her long, streaming hair in its waters. She offered sex and favor in war—and he did not turn her down. They lay together on the riverbank, and the Morrigan promised to aid the Dagda in battle and bring him the blood and kidneys of his enemy. She kept her promises. Later, the Morrigan appeared on the battlefield, chanting a powerful war poem—which frightened the opposing army so much that they were easily routed and driven into the sea.

SONGS AND POEMS OF WAR

In ancient Celtic culture, bards composed war poems to inspire warriors in battle. In ancient Ireland, this type of poem was called a *roscad*. Not all *roscada* were war poems, but many were. Music and poetry were both important parts of battle in Celtic culture. Armies went to war accompanied by massive carnyxes, huge bronze war trumpets with mouthpieces decorated to look like animals and mythological beasts. Ancient writers described the sound of a Celtic war as a terrifying cacophony that seemed to rise from the earth itself.

OYA

———◆———

PRONUNCIATION: OH-yah

AKA: Mother of Nine, Aido-Wedo, Lady of the Wind, Thunder Maiden, Goddess of the Nine Skirts, Lady of War

APPEARANCE: Oya is often depicted as a tall, strong warrior woman wearing dark red and a turban twisted into the horns of a buffalo. She dances with nine whirlwinds, wears nine voluminous skirts, and manipulates lightning.

SYMBOLS:

• **The number nine:** This is Oya's sacred number, representing the number of her children and the number of tributaries in the Niger River.

• **Buffalo:** Oya is said to be able to transform into a buffalo.

• **Lightning:** Oya has dominion over storms, wild weather, wind, and lightning.

• **Cemeteries:** Oya is said to guard the gates of cemeteries.

———◆———

Overview

Oya is a Yoruba warrior goddess, or *orisha*, with a special affinity for storms, deluges, lightning, and tornadoes. (The Yoruba are a West African ethnic group whose homeland encompasses regions of Nigeria, Benin, and Togo.) She is also prominent in the religions of Afro-Cuban, Brazilian, and other

African-diaspora regions. She is a protector of women, and those with an affinity to her are said to be strong women with natural leadership abilities.

Oya has both destructive and regenerative qualities. Her name means "the tearer," and she is capable of great devastation as both a goddess of violent weather and as a skilled, passionate warrior. She is also known for her persuasive qualities. She is said to rule over the marketplace and business—but also guards the gates of cemeteries.

She is a goddess of both destruction and regeneration. Hers is the kind of fearless destruction that precedes transformative change.

What's Her Story?

Oya's first husband was Ogun, orisha of the forge. It was an arranged marriage, and there was little love between them. Ogun was the inventor of iron weaponry and a dedicated warrior, far more comfortable among his fellow warriors than with his wife. Of course, Oya was a warrior, too, but Ogun did not like her fighting alongside him. He insisted she spend her days at home.

One day, Shango—orisha of thunder—spied Oya from afar and fell instantly in lust. He decided he *must* get to know this stunning, strong goddess. So he braided his long, sexy hair, put on his best crimson cloak, mounted his white stallion, and set out on his way.

Shango was magnificently handsome, and he was very aware of this fact. On his way, several mortals saw him and went mad at the sight of his beauty. He fully expected Oya to fall instantly to his feet. Instead, she laughed in his face.

Shango did not understand why she wasn't impressed. He was, after all, an exceedingly handsome god. But Oya looked him up and down skeptically and told him he'd have to bring more to the table than beauty to impress her.

So Shango began to seriously make his case. He swore he could blow her mind in bed, and he'd make the best husband she could ever imagine. When Oya pointed out she was already married, he swore he'd fight her husband to the death. Oya laughed and told him she was perfectly capable of fighting her own battles. Then she drew her two swords, called on her powers of wind and lightning, and proceeded to kick Shango's ass.

After recovering from his epic beatdown, Shango knew he had met his match. This woman was his soul mate. He begged her to come with him and fight alongside him in battle—and those were the magic words. Oya realized that Shango truly saw her as his equal and respected her as a warrior—*and* he was hot. But then again, so was she—they were a perfect match in every way. Oya leaped up behind Shango on his white stallion, and soon after that, they were husband and wife.

When Ogun found out his wife had left him for Shango, he vowed to get even. He spent his time building his strength and growing his army, and eventually he challenged Shango to war. Their battles were fought primarily in the forest, where Ogun was under the protection of his allies—gods of the forests and the hunt. On his home ground, Ogun was practically invincible. Shango was a strong warrior, but even he was starting to believe he might not win this one.

Now, Shango had ordered Oya to stay home and sit this one out—despite his promise to let her fight beside him. But Oya refused to obey. She followed him in secret into battle, and just as it seemed as though Shango was going to lose, she rose to her full height and began to shake out her nine billowing skirts.

A violent wind kicked up. It blew so hard that warriors, trees, and the very forest itself were blown away, scouring Ogun's domain until it became a desert. After that, Shango was easily able to defeat Ogun.

WINDS OF WEST AFRICA

From November to March, a dry season occurs in the area where the Yoruba live. The season is called Harmattan, and it is dominated by a wind of the same name. The Harmattan wind blows across West Africa from the Sahara, bringing with it dry, dusty desert air that can sometimes create a fog-like haze. On some days, the haze is so thick that flights have to be canceled due to low visibility. The wind is so dry that it sometimes causes tree branches to desiccate and break off. When it clashes with monsoon winds in the area, it can give rise to tornadoes.

Was Oya's mythology inspired by the Harmattan? It's hard to say for sure. However, the fact that she is associated with tornadoes may be a clue—as is the myth of how she defeated Ogun for Shango, in which she blew away all green and growing things and created a dry desert.

PELE

Hawaiian Goddess of Volcanoes, Fire, and Rebirth

PRONUNCIATION: PEH-leh

AKA: Madame Pele, Tūtū Pele, Pele-honua-mea ("Pele of the Sacred Land"),
Ka wahineʻai honua ("the Earth-Eating Woman"),
She Who Shapes the Sacred Land

APPEARANCE: Pele's appearance can vary greatly. Sometimes she chooses
the form of a young woman, other times an old woman. Occasionally she's
accompanied by a dog. She always wears a red muumuu.

SYMBOLS:

• **Volcanoes and lava:** Pele is strongly associated with volcanoes and lava.

• **Fire:** Pele is a fiery goddess—both literally and emotionally.
Refuse or deny her at your own peril.

• **The hula:** Pele is associated with this traditional dance because
it was first performed by her favorite sister, Hiʻiaka. Pele now has a
hula dedicated just to her (as many different Hawaiian gods and goddesses do).
The dance dedicated to Pele represents her fierce personality
and the movements of lava flows.

Overview

Pele is a powerful goddess of creation and destruction in Hawaiian culture. Polynesian mythology often involves far-traveling deities and heroes, and Pele is no exception, as she came to Hawaii from Tahiti. There are many versions of the story that explain why she made this journey. Some say that she was ambitious and, of course, fiery, and that her father feared her ambition and exiled her.

Others say that before she became a goddess, Pele seduced her brother-in-law and angered her sister, the goddess Nā-maka-o-Kahaʻi. Nā-maka-o-Kahaʻi's wrath was formidable and terrifying, and Pele was forced to flee Tahiti. But her sister followed her, and everywhere Pele stopped in the Hawaiian islands, Nā-maka-o-Kahaʻi wasn't far behind.

The first island Pele stopped at was Kauai, where Nā-maka-o-Kahaʻi attacked her and left her for dead. Pele recovered and fled to Oahu, where she dug firepits that became the Diamond Head crater. But her sister followed her there too.

Pele island-hopped to Molokai and on to Maui, where she made the Haleakala volcano. Nā-maka-o-Kahaʻi caught up with Pele again on Maui, and an epic battle commenced in which Nā-maka-o-Kahaʻi tore her sister apart. In this destruction, Pele became a goddess in her own right—and fled to the island of Hawaii, where she dug her last firepit at the summit of the volcano Kīlauea.

That's why her home is said to be the firepit Halemaʻumaʻu, which can be found at the summit of Kīlauea—the youngest and most active volcano in Hawaii and one of the most active on earth. Local legends claim that Pele still walks among its lava flows.

What's Her Story?

After Pele settled in Kīlauea, she fell into a deep sleep and left her body to travel to other islands as a spirit. While she traveled, she heard the most beautiful singing coming from the island of Kauai. She was drawn to the island and to the singer, the young chief Lohi'au.

Pele and Lohi'au had a passionate romance. They spent nine incredible days together, and they couldn't get enough of each other. But on the ninth day, Pele's sister Hi'iaka woke her up. Hi'iaka had been watching over Pele's body for nine days and worried that something was wrong when Pele hadn't woken.

Hi'iaka was Pele's most beloved sister. Pele had brought her to Hawaii as an egg while she was fleeing from Nā-maka-o-Kaha'i. During all those desperate flights and vicious battles, she had incubated the egg, keeping it warm in her armpit. Hi'iaka was the first person to dance the hula and became the patron and goddess of the hula. She was also Pele's best friend and confidante.

Hi'iaka knew as soon as Pele woke up that something was wrong. Pele was in love with Lohi'au, and she was volatile and angry that she wasn't with him. Pele asked Hi'iaka, the only person she trusted, to bring Lohi'au to her. She also made Hi'iaka swear not to fall in love with him herself.

Hi'iaka promised she wouldn't fall in love with the young chief. But when she traveled to his island, she found him dead—he had wasted away pining for Pele. Hi'iaka was able to resurrect him, and the two returned to Pele. But, unfortunately, Hi'iaka broke her promise to her sister not to fall in love with the young man herself.

Some stories say that Hi'iaka and Lohi'au fell in love more or less at first sight. Others say that their love affair didn't begin until after they returned to Pele. But most stories agree that Pele was furious about this betrayal. She killed Lohi'au with a lava flow, only to have Hi'iaka resurrect him again.

Some tales say that after his second resurrection, Lohiʻau was able to choose his own fate. In some versions, he chose to stay with Hiʻiaka; in others, he decided to remain with both sisters in a polyamorous relationship. In other versions of the tale, he returned to his island alone.

PELE IN MODERN FOLK LEGENDS

There are many modern urban legends about the goddess Pele. Wherever Pele is seen, disaster is about to follow. Stories claim that those who stop to speak to Pele or offer her a ride are spared and given a warning about impending doom. Those who do not heed her warnings, or who don't stop to help her, often meet with a bad end. There are also modern tales of tourists who have taken volcanic rocks from Hawaii only to find that bad fortune has followed them. Some believe that this is because Pele has cursed them for removing the rocks, as they are pieces of Pele, parts of her body that make up the sacred island. Every year tourists mail rocks back to Hawaii, apologizing for stealing from Pele.

There are also legends about the red ʻohelo berries that grow along the edges of Halemaʻumaʻu crater. It is bad luck to eat these berries without first making an offering to Pele or asking her permission.

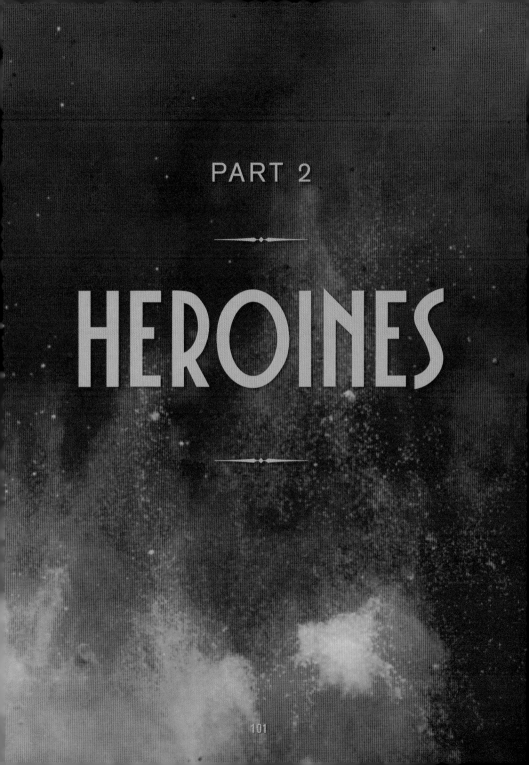

PART 2

HEROINES

AMBA/SHIKHANDI

Vengeance-Seeking
Genderqueer Warrior of the *Mahabharata*

———◆———

PRONUNCIATION: AHM-buh / Shee-KHAN-dee

APPEARANCE: Amba is generally described as a beautiful cisgender woman.
Shikhandi may be depicted as a man, a woman, or androgynous.

———◆———

Overview

Amba and Shikhandi are two different incarnations of the same character from the *Mahabharata*, an ancient epic poem from India. Amba, the earlier incarnation, is a cisgender woman. Her later incarnation, Shikhandi, has a more complicated gender identity. In some versions of the tale, Shikhandi is depicted as a transgender man. He is assigned female at birth but identifies as male and later swaps genitals with a forest spirit to gain male genitals.

However, some interpretations of Shikhandi represent the character as a trans woman—born or transformed into a body assigned male but retaining Amba's memories, personality, identity, and all-consuming drive for revenge. In some tellings, Shikhandi is a cisgender woman who trains as a warrior—a role that was then usually assigned to men. In this way, cisgender Shikhandi still defies traditional gender roles.

In all versions of the story, Shikhandi's gender transcends the binary, reflecting the fact that in the ancient world, just as today, transgender and genderqueer people lived and loved passionately and fiercely—and took epic revenge against their enemies.

The story of Amba and Shikhandi is not as common in popular culture as other stories from the *Mahabharata*, but it is slowly gaining more attention. Two TV series were made that told the story of the *Mahabharata*; both were called *Mahabharat*. One aired from 1988–1990 and the other from 2013–2014. Both included the story of Amba and Shikhandi. More recently, in 2019, the Chennai-based theater group Veshadharis produced a play about the lives of Amba and Shikhandi, entitled *Shikhandi: A Story of Revenge from Mahabharata*.

What's Their Story?

Amba was born a cisgender woman, the daughter of the king of Kashi. She was the eldest of three daughters, and when her father decided it was time for her and her sisters to marry, he planned to throw them a *swayamvara*—an event where a woman chooses her husband out of a number of eligible suitors.

Amba was secretly in love with Salva, the king of Salwa—and promised that she would choose him at the *swayamvara*. But the undefeatable warrior Bhishma heard that three very eligible princesses were looking for husbands, so he decided to sweep in and kidnap all three of them as wives for his stepbrother—whether they liked it or not. (They didn't.)

So on the day of the *swayamvara*, Bhishma rolled up and declared that he would be taking the princesses now. He fought off all attackers, wounding Amba's love interest, Salva, in a duel. Then he took the princesses home and started planning a wedding ceremony for all three of them and his stepbrother.

Amba flat-out refused to marry the stepbrother. She cursed Bhishma out and told him that she was in love with Salva, she was planning to marry him, and Bhishma had messed it all up for her. Bhishma, feeling a bit sheepish, decided to send her back to Salva with an apology note. But when Amba showed up in Salwa, Salva rejected her because she'd been kidnapped by another man, making her damaged goods. Plus, he wasn't over the humiliation of Bhishma defeating him in a duel.

Amba was furious. At Salva, sure, but especially at Bhishma, who had casually ruined her life and reputation, making it impossible for her to marry at all. He even refused to marry her himself to fix the problem he'd caused. Rude.

So Amba decided she was going to wreck Bhishma's life the way he had wrecked hers. But Bhishma was a very powerful warrior, and everyone feared him. Amba knew she couldn't take him down alone. She tried to get allies on her side, but other kings refused to help her out of fear of Bhishma. Finally, Amba went to the forest and prayed for the gods to grant her a boon to help her utterly destroy him.

The god Shiva appeared and told her that she would destroy Bhishma, but only in her next life—however, she would remember her life as Amba and her mission of vengeance in the next one. So Amba promptly built herself a funeral pyre and jumped into it, hastening her own rebirth. According to some versions of the tale, Amba was reborn and took her own life many times until she was reincarnated in a life where she would be able to slay Bhishma.

Eventually, Amba was reborn as Shikhandi—child of King Drupada and elder sibling of the heroine Draupadi and her twin brother. In this version of the tale, Shikhandi was assigned female at birth, but the god Shiva told Drupada that the baby girl would later transform into a boy. So Drupada decided to raise Shikhandi as a boy.

Shikhandi grew up and got engaged to a princess of Dasharna. Not long after their wedding, the princess told everyone that Shikhandi was really a woman—an egregious misgendering that started a war. Shikhandi fled to the forest, planning to fast to death out of shame. But in the forest, Shikhandi met a yaksha—or forest spirit—who offered to swap sexes. The yaksha offered male genitals in exchange for Shikhandi's female genitals, and Shikhandi agreed.

Shikhandi trained to become a great warrior, and during the Kurukshetra War, he sided with the Pandavas—the five husbands of Draupadi. (You can get more background on them and the Kurukshetra War in the entry on Draupadi later in this part.) He became the charioteer of the Pandava prince Arjuna, husband of Draupadi.

During battle, Arjuna and Shikhandi encountered Bhishma, who was fighting with the opposing army. As soon as he saw Shikhandi, Bhishma knew his time had come. He lowered his weapons and died, pierced many times by a barrage of arrows from Shikhandi and Arjuna.

THE THIRD GENDER

On the Indian subcontinent, some identify as a third gender—neither man nor woman. The third gender has an ancient history in India. It's discussed in the *Kama Sutra*, parts of which may date back as far as the 400s B.C. Today, many live in intentional communities of third-gender residents that have existed for generations.

It's quite possible that Shikhandi can be most accurately identified as this gender. People who identify as the third gender may be queer or gender nonconforming in a variety of ways, including gender-fluid, transgender, nonbinary, or intersex.

In 2014, India's supreme court granted the third gender an official status. Residents can claim it as their gender identity on official documents, and the law recognizes them as a marginalized group and offers certain protections. However, people who identify as the third gender still face a great deal of discrimination, especially in more conservative areas of the country.

ARAWELO

Legendary Somali Queen Who Smashed the Patriarchy

PRONUNCIATION: AH-ra-WEH-loh

AKA: Arraweelo, Moroombe, Caraweelo

APPEARANCE: Legend says that Arawelo was beautiful, but there are few specific details about what she looked like.

Overview

Arawelo is a legendary Somali queen who defied traditional gender roles and overturned the patriarchy in her realm, installing women in positions of societal power and assigning men to the roles of homelife and child-rearing.

Arawelo is a popular folk heroine in Somali culture, but it's unclear when or if she really existed. However, the legend says that she grew up in a strongly patriarchal, feudal society and that she witnessed many injustices against women before she became queen herself. She also grew up watching the men around her start wars with no concern for the death toll. When she became queen, she appointed women to positions of power in her own government as part of a strategy for ensuring a peaceful reign.

Some versions of her story state that she actively oppressed men and encouraged others to do the same, training women to lash out aggressively against the men in their families and ordering the castration of any men who disobeyed her laws. These legends may have arisen after Arawelo's death to demonize female leaders and justify reinstatement of patriarchal control.

Today, Arawelo is a popular name for Somali girls. It's also sometimes used as a nickname for confident girls and women with leadership qualities.

What's Her Story?

Arawelo was born into a royal family without sons. As the eldest of three daughters, she was next in line for the throne. Arawelo demonstrated leadership qualities—and a penchant for utterly ignoring traditional gender roles—long before she became queen. During a period of profound drought, she assembled a team of women to hunt and gather water to keep their town supplied and prevent a mass migration.

These were traditionally men's activities, but Arawelo ignored any naysayers who insisted she couldn't hunt and find water as a woman. She and her friends just kept out-hunting the guys and proving the haters wrong.

Eventually, Arawelo's father died and she inherited the throne. She also got married. Her husband tried to get Arawelo to embrace her expected duties as a woman—pressuring her to focus on raising kids and tending the home and urging her to leave the hard work of ruling the country to him.

Arawelo refused. She didn't believe women *should* restrict themselves to child-rearing and the home, even though that was what everyone expected. In defiance of her husband, Arawelo put out a call for all women in her kingdom to essentially go on strike—to abandon all childcare and home-making and start taking power outside the home.

Eventually, men were forced to take a larger role in child-rearing and domestic duties, because the women in Arawelo's kingdom rejected these roles. But Arawelo didn't stop there. She embarked on a project to transform her country into an entirely matriarchal one, where women were the primary breadwinners and leaders outside the home.

A keen observer of human nature, Arawelo noticed that men were usually the instigators in war. Men started wars, men continued wars, and men made wars worse. She believed women were much more levelheaded, were better rulers, and were more effective diplomats. Thus, she fired all her generals, diplomats, and politicians who were men and appointed women in positions of power. Arawelo implemented other reforms, too, such as making sure girls in her kingdom got the same education as boys.

Sometimes, Arawelo is depicted as not just being committed to gender equality, but as actively oppressing men. In one version of her story, she trained women to inflict violence on the men in their lives and even ordered the widespread castration of men in her kingdom so they wouldn't reproduce. Other legends say that she used to hang rapists by their testicles.

Another version of the myth states that Arawelo didn't commit targeted violence against men but that she allowed these rumors to spread so that men would think twice about disobeying her laws—specifically laws about violent aggression and instigating wars. This was one way she maintained peace in her kingdom.

It's not clear how Queen Arawelo died. One story says that she was murdered by a grandson who wanted to reinstate patriarchal control over women. Another says that she was assassinated while attending the funeral of a friend.

It's not certain when she lived, how she died, or even whether she existed at all. However, Arawelo's legend lives on in the strong Somali women who bear her name.

WHERE WAS ARAWELO'S KINGDOM?

There is little evidence that Arawelo was a real historical figure. However, her kingdom is often said to have been located in the Sanaag region of northeastern Somalia. Some accounts suggest a date of around A.D. 15 for her reign—making her story more than two thousand years old. There is a large stone tumulus in the Sanaag region that is associated with Arawelo in folklore. According to legend, the tumulus is her grave and all that remains of her ancient realm.

Other legends suggest that she was a queen of the Harla people. The Harla lived throughout the Horn of Africa and established their own state, the Harla Kingdom, around the sixth century A.D. The Harla Kingdom was quite advanced, with extensive trade contacts and its own calendar and currency. Many ruins from its culture, including mosques, houses, cave paintings, monuments, tumuli, and necropolises, can still be seen today in Djibouti, Somalia, and Ethiopia.

ATALANTA

Ancient Greek Warrior, Athlete, and Argonaut

PRONUNCIATION: AT-a-LAN-ta

AKA: Swift-Footed

APPEARANCE: Atalanta was a fair and fierce young woman with golden hair. She was as terrifying as she was beautiful—she was able to instill fear in men. She is often depicted dressed similarly to Artemis, with a bow and arrow.

SYMBOLS:
- None, but she is strongly associated with bears, lions, golden apples, archery, the goddess Artemis, and the hunt for the Calydonian boar.

Overview

Greek mythology doesn't have many heroines who go on epic quests, battle men (and centaurs), and live off the grid. Atalanta, whose name means "equal in weight" (in other words, equal to any man), is one of the few women of Greek mythology who took on male warriors and hunters—and won. Atalanta is the only female Argonaut—the epic band of ancient Greek heroes including Heracles, Jason, Orpheus, Castor, and Polydeuces (Pollux)—who went on the quest to find the Golden Fleece.

Atalanta was born to the king and queen of Arkadía, a mountainous area in the central Peloponnese. But Atalanta's father was not interested in having a female child. So Atalanta was "exposed" as an infant—meaning, left out in the woods to die from starvation, cold, or wild animal attacks. This was a common way the ancient Greeks dealt with unwanted pregnancies. Girls were in particular danger of exposure.

In her story, Atalanta was found by a friendly bear, who suckled her and raised her to hunt and fight like a bear. As she grew older, Atalanta was taken in by some woman hunters who were followers of Artemis, the goddess of the hunt. They taught her to be an exceptional huntress—particularly skilled with a bow and arrow.

Atalanta swore to devote herself to the goddess Artemis and remain a virgin. According to the Roman author Ovid, Atalanta was warned that terrible things would happen to her if she lost her virginity.

Atalanta slew two centaurs who tried to attack her. She wrestled Peleus (Achilles's dad, who was famous for one thing: wrestling) and beat him. And she also drew the first blood during the Calydonian boar hunt and fell in love with the tragic hero Meleager.

In modern times, you might see Atalanta in film and comics. Some examples include the movie *Hercules* (2014), the *Incredible Hulk* comics, and video games such as *Zeus: Master of Olympus*, *Rise of the Argonauts*, and *Age of Mythology*.

What's Her Story?

Atalanta's most famous story involves a footrace and her desire to only marry a man who is her equal—which is revolutionary for Greek mythology. After stories of Atalanta's heroic exploits reached her father's ears, he decided that having a famous daughter might not be a bad thing. So he decided, after exposing her at birth and subsequently ignoring her for her entire life, to claim her as his own.

We don't know how Atalanta felt about this, but we do know that she reconciled with her father. As soon as they made up, her father decided it was long past time for his daughter to be married and produce some exceptional heirs (or some such patriarchal nonsense). Atalanta went along with her father's plan, but she had a stipulation. She would only marry someone who could beat her in a footrace. And if they couldn't beat her, she got to kill them. She wanted to marry someone who was her equal, not just someone who had a lot of money and power.

Her father agreed to this request. Any man who wanted to marry Atalanta would have to bring a hefty dowry *and* beat her in a footrace. Atalanta's father saw this as a win for him.

Atalanta chose to run the race in her full armor (because she was a badass), which gave her opponents a significant advantage. This was her not-so-subtle way of showing those who wanted to challenge her that she was not just their equal but their superior. Man after man came to race her, and all of them lost. Legends of her beauty and fierceness grew throughout the ancient world along with her fame.

Then along came Hippomenes. He fell in love with Atalanta at first sight, but the feeling was not mutual. Desperate to win the hand of Atalanta, he prayed to Aphrodite, the goddess of love and desire, for help. She gifted him three golden apples from the Garden of the Hesperides—but made him promise that once he won the race, he would give proper thanks (and tribute) to her.

These were the apples of heroes—the apples that Heracles had gone to the edge of the world to find. These divine apples were a symbol of everything Atalanta aspired to. Without these apples, Hippomenes would have been just another slaughtered suitor. But with them, he managed to best Atalanta. During the race, every time Atalanta pulled ahead, Hippomenes would strategically drop one of the apples. Atalanta found them irresistible, and each time he dropped an apple, Atalanta veered off track and chased it.

Eventually, Hippomenes won the race, but not by beating her fair and square. Even so, Atalanta had to marry him. But even if their relationship started off rocky, they wound up *really* liking each other—so much that they became one of those annoying PDA couples.

Ovid said this was because Hippomenes forgot to pay tribute to Aphrodite and she cursed the couple with lust. But it's also possible that Atalanta had finally found her equal, and she actually loved him. Either way, their PDA got them into trouble one day when they were off hunting. They found a temple to Cybele and wound up, um, "desecrating" it. As punishment, Cybele turned them into lions and forced them to pull her chariot.

The ancient Greeks believed that lions could not mate with each other—they could only mate with leopards. But the joke was on them, because lions obviously mate with other lions. So immortal lions Atalanta and Hippomenes are very likely still out there somewhere, hunting, living off the grid, still in love, and still engaging in way too much PDA.

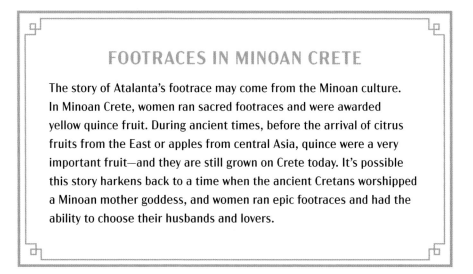

FOOTRACES IN MINOAN CRETE

The story of Atalanta's footrace may come from the Minoan culture. In Minoan Crete, women ran sacred footraces and were awarded yellow quince fruit. During ancient times, before the arrival of citrus fruits from the East or apples from central Asia, quince were a very important fruit—and they are still grown on Crete today. It's possible this story harkens back to a time when the ancient Cretans worshipped a Minoan mother goddess, and women ran epic footraces and had the ability to choose their husbands and lovers.

PRINCESS BARI

Korean Shaman Who Moved Between Worlds

PRONUNCIATION: PRIN-cess BAH-ree

AKA: Barigongju

SYMBOLS:

• **The Big Dipper:** She is said to rule over the constellation the Big Dipper, also known as Ch'ilsong or the Spirit of the Seven Stars in Korean tradition.

Overview

Princess Bari is the seventh daughter of a king and queen in Korean legend and shamanic religious belief who was abandoned at birth because she was a girl. When grown to adulthood, she traveled to the underworld to retrieve a healing flower or medicinal waters to save her ailing parents.

There are more than a hundred versions of this story tied to various localities in Korea. Broadly, it tells of the origins of a goddess of the underworld, although the nature of her divinity varies by region and tradition—and in some traditions, she never becomes a goddess at all.

Princess Bari is also considered a patron goddess of Korean shamans. Her story is traditionally sung during shamanic funerary rituals. The novel *Princess Bari* by Hwang Sok-yong tells the story of her life.

What's Her Story?

The story begins with a king and queen who were very much in love and planned to marry. According to one version, they were admonished by an influential shaman not to marry too quickly, but they didn't listen and married as soon as they could. This proved inauspicious.

Because of their transgression, the couple had six daughters and no sons. When the queen got pregnant a seventh time, she had a favorable dream, which was interpreted to mean that the seventh child would be a son. To the king and queen's great consternation, the dream turned out to be wrong. They had another daughter.

The king was so angry that he abandoned the seventh daughter in the woods—which was how she got the name Bari, which means "thrown away." Princess Bari did not die in the woods, however. She was rescued and raised—by helpful animals, local mountain gods, kind peasants, or the Buddha, depending on the version.

Years after abandoning their daughter, the king and queen fell gravely ill. There was only one cure for their sickness—powerful healing flowers (or, in some versions, medicinal waters) that could be found only in the realm of the dead.

The king ordered each of his six daughters to go to the underworld to retrieve these flowers. But each of the daughters refused to make the dangerous journey. So the king searched far and wide to find his abandoned daughter. Finally, Princess Bari was found and brought from the wilderness, where her parents persuaded her to go and find this healing flower.

Princess Bari traveled to the underworld, dressing as a man for her own protection. In some versions—the western Korean version has a strong Buddhist influence—she met the Buddha after going three thousand leagues on her journey, and he asked her if she had it in her to make this terrible journey, considering she was a woman. When Princess Bari answered that she would continue the journey even if it killed her, he offered her a silk flower, which she used to transform an endless, uncrossable ocean into dry land.

Finally, Princess Bari reached the place where the healing flower could be found, but she didn't have the herbal knowledge to discern which could heal her parents. The place was guarded by a magical being—in some versions a monster, in others an exiled god. Bari decided to stay with the magical guardian. She married him and bore him sons, and in return he taught her the herbology of the underworld.

Slowly, she developed the knowledge of which flowers and herbs would save her parents. Eventually, she traveled back to the world of the living, only to find that she was too late—her parents had already died of their illness.

But all was not lost. Bari appeared at their funeral, opened their coffins, and raised them from the dead with the healing flower. It was then that she became a goddess.

KOREAN SHAMANISM

Some versions of the Princess Bari story carry a strong Buddhist influence. But even so, at its core, this is an origin story for the ancient shamanistic religion of Korea, which is still practiced today. The shamanistic tradition may date back as far as three thousand years or more on the Korean peninsula. It includes the worship of ancestors, nature spirits, and an expansive pantheon of gods and goddesses. Shamans serve as intermediaries to the spirit world through the practice of special rituals called *gut* rituals. Modern-day shamans can be men or women, but in its most ancient form, the religion was primarily led by women. Traditionally, these were women of lower social status who did not have a lot of power or influence within the strict Confucian feudalist culture of the time. The shamanistic religion gave them a strong voice and influence within their communities.

DIDO

PRONUNCIATION: DY-doh

AKA: Elissa, Alyssa, Queen of Carthage, Elishat, Elisha,
Alashiya, the Wanderer, Beloved

SYMBOLS:
• **The city of Carthage:** Dido's legacy is strong in Tunisia,
where the women of the country are sometimes called "the daughters of Dido."
She is seen as a national symbol and has been featured on their money.

Overview

Dido is a pseudo-historical figure whose name means "wanderer." She learned how to use a sword from Scythian warrior women, ruled as queen, led her people in migration, and founded a new city. Dido first appeared in the writings of Timaeus, a Greek historian who lived around 350–260 B.C. However, his original writings are lost and what we know of Dido is from later writers who are quoting or citing his works.

Dido's story begins in Phoenicia, where she was ruling as queen in Tyre alongside her husband. When her husband died, her brother Pygmalion took over. At first, Dido was fine with this transfer of power—until one night, the ghost of her husband appeared to her in a dream, telling her he had been murdered! By Pygmalion! Plot twist.

So Dido and a band of loyal followers fled Tyre and made their way west across the Mediterranean. They stopped at Cyprus, where they met with priests and followers of Aphrodite and invited them to join their party of refugees and found a temple to their goddess in a new city. The followers of Aphrodite were mostly women, with independence and sexual agency—a novelty in the ancient world and the perfect addition to Dido's band of exiles.

When Dido arrived in Libya, she found there were two reigning powers in the region—the neighboring Phoenician colony of Utica and King Hiarbas of Libya. She knew she had to establish her own foothold in the area and make sure it was secure. So she made a deal with King Hiarbas, offering him the treasure she had taken with her from Tyre in exchange for land from his kingdom to found a city.

King Hiarbas agreed but, thinking he could trick Dido, told her that she could only have a portion of land that could be covered by an oxhide. So Dido cut an oxhide into incredibly thin strips, thin enough to stretch for miles if laid end to end. Using the sea as a natural barrier, she laid the oxhide strips down to stake out a generous territory—and then founded the great city of Carthage. The city's citadel was named Byrsa Hill, *byrsa* meaning "oxhide," in honor of Dido's clever strategy.

Dido has inspired many plays, operas, songs, novels, and poems. But it is often because of her tragic love story with Aeneas that Dido is remembered. That story was told in *The Aeneid*, which repurposed her legend to further aggrandize the Romans and promote Augustinian values. But before the Romans co-opted her story to make her a supporting character in Aeneas's tale, Dido was a strong queen who founded a city that would rival Rome, standing up to the men who wanted to cheat and oppress her.

What's Her Story?

The fiercely intelligent, determined, and independent Dido swore never to marry again and to rule as a queen in her own right. No matter how many suitors tried to court her, she always turned them away—until the gods intervened.

Dido's most famous appearance is in Virgil's epic Roman poem *The Aeneid* (29–19 B.C.). *The Aeneid* was written during Rome's evolution from republic to empire, and its purpose was to give the Romans their own ancient epic to rival *The Iliad* or *The Odyssey*—and to give Octavian, better known as Augustus, legitimacy as Rome's new ruler. The Romans were a new empire, and they wanted to get their hands on some of that old-world mythological cachet.

Dido appeared in *The Aeneid* as a romantic interest for the Trojan hero Aeneas. Aeneas, his father, and his son fled the burning city of Troy and were tasked by Jupiter to found a great city in Italy (which would later become Rome). On his way to founding this city, Aeneas visited Carthage and met with Dido. At first, Dido was not at all interested in Aeneas. And that's where the gods intervened.

Venus, the mother of Aeneas, tasked her son Cupid with shooting a love arrow at Dido and making her fall hopelessly in love with Aeneas. It worked. Dido was stricken with insatiable love for the traveling hero. They got it on, and later they got married in a sexy private cave ceremony.

But the gods had other plans for Aeneas. Mercury, the messenger of the gods, appeared to him in a dream and told him he needed to get moving. He was supposed to be founding his own great city—not resting on the laurels of another city, one founded by Dido. So Aeneas told Dido he had to go, and Dido was heartbroken. She offered to let Aeneas rule with her and share power. But Aeneas did not change his mind. He gathered up his men, and they prepared their ships and left in the dead of night.

Dido was well aware of what Aeneas was planning. She had a huge pyre built on a hill. The pyre was so big and the flames so bright that it could not be missed—even from way out at sea. She climbed upon the pyre and stabbed herself with a sword, cursing Aeneas and his people for all eternity. She commanded her people and their ancestors to "rise up from [her] bones, avenging spirit." And then she jumped into the flames.

And from 264–146 B.C., the people of Carthage rose up against Rome in a series of bloody battles called the Punic Wars, later said to be caused by Dido's mythical curse.

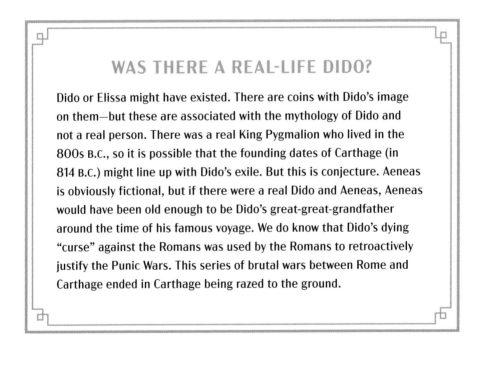

WAS THERE A REAL-LIFE DIDO?

Dido or Elissa might have existed. There are coins with Dido's image on them—but these are associated with the mythology of Dido and not a real person. There was a real King Pygmalion who lived in the 800s B.C., so it is possible that the founding dates of Carthage (in 814 B.C.) might line up with Dido's exile. But this is conjecture. Aeneas is obviously fictional, but if there were a real Dido and Aeneas, Aeneas would have been old enough to be Dido's great-great-grandfather around the time of his famous voyage. We do know that Dido's dying "curse" against the Romans was used by the Romans to retroactively justify the Punic Wars. This series of brutal wars between Rome and Carthage ended in Carthage being razed to the ground.

DRAUPADI

Fire-Born Heroine of the *Mahabharata*

PRONUNCIATION: DROH-puh-dee

AKA: Krishnaa, Panchali, Yajnaseni, Nityayuvani, Malini, Panchavallabha

APPEARANCE: Draupadi is described in the *Mahabharata* as extremely beautiful—
with a dark complexion; large, dark eyes; nails like shining copper;
and curly dark hair.

Overview

Draupadi is a central character in the *Mahabharata*, an ancient Hindu epic that may have been written between 400 B.C. and A.D. 400—though some scholars believe its origins date closer to the ninth century B.C. She is described as the most beautiful woman in all of creation. She was born in fire, brought into being from a *yajna*, or fire sacrifice, performed by a father bent on creating a child as an instrument of revenge.

In the *Mahabharata*, it was prophesied that Draupadi would bring about the doom of many brave warriors. This turned out to be true in a sense, as events that led to the Kurukshetra War, one of the most important conflicts in the epic, hinged around her.

Draupadi was the wife of five brothers—one of the very few examples in ancient Sanskrit writings of a polyandrous marriage. She was an empress in her own right, said to rule with wisdom and compassion. But she was also fiery and vengeful. Some versions of her myth hold that during the Kurukshetra War, she washed her hair in the blood of her enemies as an act of vengeance.

Draupadi's story has captivated audiences throughout the centuries, and she has appeared as a central character in numerous plays, TV shows, novels, traditional dances, and other performances in languages including Hindi, Tamil, Marathi, Kannada, and more.

Among many other movies and TV shows, Draupadi is featured prominently in both the live-action *Mahabharat* TV series as well as an animated movie of the same name. The first film produced in South India, *Keechaka Vadham*—produced in 1917, features her as a main character. More recently, the 2019 Kannada-language film *Kurukshetra* includes her story.

Among many literary adaptations, Draupadi has been featured in the novel *Yajnaseni: The Story of Draupadi* by Moortidevi Award–winning author Pratibha Ray, in Chitra Banerjee Divakaruni's novel *The Palace of Illusions*, and in the Sahitya Akademi Award–winning novel *Draupadi* by Yarlagadda Lakshmi Prasad, which reimagines the events of the *Mahabharata* from Draupadi's point of view.

What's Her Story?

When Draupadi's father, King Drupada, lost half his kingdom to an enemy who was once a childhood friend, he swore vengeance—but he knew he wasn't strong enough to carry it out himself. So he performed a fire ritual, or *yajna*, to create a child who could rain destruction on his enemies.

Two children walked out of the fire. The first was Dhrishtadyumna, a son who would prove a capable warrior. The second was an astonishingly beautiful daughter named Draupadi, who was prophesied to bring about cataclysmic destruction. Somehow, this prophecy didn't put off suitors.

News traveled that this stunningly beautiful woman was *single*, and soon hundreds of men were traveling to King Drupada's palace to win her hand in marriage. There were so many that Drupada decided to make it a real competition. Each suitor had to lift and string a massive bow, then pierce the eye of a golden fish with an arrow—by looking only at its reflection in a pool.

Among those who came to win Draupadi's hand were the Pandavas—five brothers who were actually exiled princes disguised as Brahmans. One of them, Arjuna, effortlessly succeeded in this difficult task. He won Draupadi's hand, and she was thrilled. She liked him too.

The other suitors, however, were *not* thrilled. There were kings and princes among them, and they resented losing to someone who wasn't royal (at least, as far as they knew). The Pandavas wound up having to fight their way out of Drupada's palace.

The boys fought off the other suitors, escaped to the forest with Draupadi, and rushed home, bursting into the cabin they shared with their mother. Arjuna shouted, "Look what we found!" And their mom, without looking up from what she was doing, told Arjuna that whatever it was, he'd better share with his brothers.

Of course, a mother's word is law. So Arjuna and his four brothers all married Draupadi.

Eventually, the Pandavas came out of exile. This didn't go over well with the Kauravas, the faction of their family currently in power. This was especially true for their cousin Duryodhana and their uncle Dhritarashtra, who had been ruling as crown prince and king (respectively) in their stead.

King Dhritarashtra, uncle of the Pandavas and father of the Kauravas, proposed dividing the kingdom among them and assigned the Pandavas a desert wasteland. They transformed it into a rich and thriving kingdom called Indraprastha, and Draupadi ruled there as queen—managing the treasury and developing a reputation as a wise and competent ruler.

But the Kauravas were consumed with jealousy. Cousin Duryodhana and his uncle Shakuni challenged the brothers to a dice game, hoping to make them lose everything. According to some legends, Duryodhana's uncle Shakuni had magical dice that could never lose, made from the bones of his own father.

Either the dice really were magical or the Pandavas were absolutely terrible at dice—especially the eldest, Yudhishthira. He lost everything, eventually betting all his brothers and himself into slavery. Duryodhana told Yudhishthira that he could get himself and his brothers out of slavery if he was willing to wager Draupadi in the next round. Desperate, Yudhishthira agreed. He lost that round too.

Duryodhana ordered his brother Dushasana to go find Draupadi and drag her to court by her hair, whereupon he and the other Kauravas assaulted and humiliated her in front of her husbands. Draupadi was outraged. She fiercely condemned her husbands for failing to protect her and demanded to know what right Yudhishthira had as a husband to bet her in a dice game anyway—given that he had lost everything prior to making that bet, including his station in life, while she still ranked as a queen.

Finally, Duryodhana tried to strip her naked to humiliate her further, and the god Krishna himself had to step in to stop the abuse. This set in motion the events that led to the Kurukshetra War. Some versions say that Draupadi washed her hair in Dushasana's blood, in vengeance for his treatment of her during the dice game.

WAS THERE A REAL KURUKSHETRA WAR?

Despite lasting only eighteen days, the Kurukshetra War is one of the most important events of the *Mahabharata*. Its chapters are believed to be some of the oldest in the epic. The Kurukshetra War is described as a cataclysmic battle involving magical weapons that have intrigued generations of historians—and sparked the imagination of conspiracy theorists. Some have drawn parallels between the mythic weapons in the *Mahabharata* and modern advanced weaponry, such as guided missiles and atomic bombs. But despite the fantastical events and weapons, some researchers believe that the Kurukshetra War may have some basis in history. The site of the battle is Kurukshetra—a real ancient city in northern India.

It's possible that the events of the *Mahabharata* represent a mythologized depiction of a real conflict that had a significant cultural impact in this region. Proposed dates range from the 5500s to the 900s B.C. and are based on literary, astronomical, calendrical, and archaeological evidence.

LAGERTHA

Legendary Viking Shield-Maiden

PRONUNCIATION: LA-ger-tha

AKA: Lathgertha, Ladgertha, Ladgerda

APPEARANCE: Lagertha was said to be slight of frame but had equal skill and courage to a male warrior.

Overview

Lagertha is a legendary Viking shield-maiden (see sidebar) who eventually became the ruler of Norway. She was also, briefly, the wife of Ragnar Lodbrok ("Hairy Breeches"), another prominent figure in Viking legend who appears in Icelandic sagas, Old Norse poetry, and pseudo-historical chronicles.

In 1789, the Norwegian and Danish novelist Christen Pram wrote a historical drama about her, *Lagertha*, based on the original account by Saxo Grammaticus. A couple of years later, ballet choreographer Vincenzo Galeotti created a very successful ballet of the same name. Lagertha is also a main character in the TV show *Vikings*, where she is depicted as a badass warrior, a chieftain and general, and Ragnar's first wife—who later becomes a queen herself.

What's Her Story?

Lagertha first appears in the *Gesta Danorum*, a twelfth-century document by the Christian scribe and historian Saxo Grammaticus. From there, we hear that she was in the household of Siward, king of Norway. When Frø, the king of Sweden, invaded Norway, he killed King Siward—and, because he was the worst, sent the women of Siward's household to work in a brothel against their will.

Siward's grandson Ragnar Lodbrok came to Norway at the head of a Danish army to avenge Siward's death. Along the way, he freed the women in the brothel. They joined his army, dressing as men and fighting fiercely with swords and other weapons. Among them, one warrior stood out for her exceptional bravery: Lagertha. She was always at the front lines where the fighting was fiercest, her hair loose and flying about her shoulders.

Her courage and skill with weapons caught Ragnar's eye—he even gave her credit later for winning the entire battle. He began courting her, and at first Lagertha was kind of indifferent. When he came to visit her at her home, Lagertha set her pets on him—a great hound and a bear. Ragnar killed them both, which should have been a red flag.

However, for some reason, Lagertha decided she liked him okay after that. They got married, and Lagertha had three kids with him—two daughters and a son. Ragnar and Lagertha lived together happily for several years. However, eventually his past caught up with him. Denmark exploded into civil war, and Ragnar was called back to fight.

While there, he divorced Lagertha and married someone else. The excuse he gave was that she set her dog and bear on him back when they first met, and he still wasn't over it.

Lagertha took it in stride and immediately married someone else. But, for reasons none of her friends understood, she still had a thing for Ragnar. And when he asked his friends in Norway for help fighting his war in

GRAVES OF VIKING SHIELD-MAIDENS

Lagertha was a character of legend. But Viking shield-maidens may have been real. Shield-maidens are women warriors in Scandinavian mythology. They figure prominently in Viking sagas as well as the legends of the Goths, Marcomanni, Cimbri, and other ancient Germanic cultures that were precursors to the Vikings. They also appear in Viking myths, as the wild Valkyries who carry the souls of dead warriors off to Valhalla.

Graves have been found in Scandinavia that include weapons, armor, board games used for planning out war strategy, and the bones of horses as well as people. Bones initially assumed to be male have been found to be female after closer, contemporary analysis.

For example, in the 1980s, a mass Viking grave was found in England that contained almost three hundred people. Scientists believe that this grave may be the remains of the "Great Heathen Army," which invaded England in A.D. 865. It was led by three "sons" of Ragnar Lodbrok (who weren't actually his sons, because Ragnar was fictional—that's just what the "sons" told everybody). One of these "sons of Ragnar Lodbrok" was the memorably named Ivar the Boneless. Most of the occupants of the grave were between the ages of eighteen and forty-five and had suffered violent injuries—suggesting they were warriors who died in battle. More recent analysis has found that 20 percent of the skeletons in the grave were biologically female.

Denmark, she came herself—at the head of a mighty navy of 120 Viking ships. She was instrumental in helping Ragnar win the war, bravely leading her warriors in a rear attack that routed the enemy.

Then Lagertha went back home to Norway, killed her second husband with a spearhead she'd been hiding in her dress for this exact purpose, and then took over his throne—because she preferred to rule by herself rather than share power with her husband.

MAEVE

Celtic Warrior Queen and Nemesis of Heroes

PRONUNCIATION: mayve

AKA: Méibh, Meadhbh, Méabh

APPEARANCE: Maeve is generally depicted as a beautiful golden-haired woman; her hair is as gold as intoxicating mead.

SYMBOLS:

• **Mead:** Her name is derived from the Proto-Celtic word for "mead," and it may mean "mead woman" or "one who intoxicates."

• **Wolves:** One ancient Irish poem refers to her as the "fair-haired wolf queen," whose beauty is so great it robs men of their valor.

Overview

Maeve is the queen of Connaught in the Ulster cycle, a collection of Irish legends, poems, and tales centering around the kingdoms of Ulster, Connaught, and the surrounding region of northeastern Ireland. Maeve was beautiful, wealthy, a fierce warrior and general, and sexually promiscuous. She was the enemy of Conchobar, king of Ulster, and nemesis of Cuchulainn, the hero of the Ulster cycle.

Maeve's character may have arisen from a more ancient Irish woman of myth: Medb Lethderg, a sovereignty goddess who ruled over Tara, the hill where Irish High Kings were crowned.

Legend has it that Medb Lethderg had married or slept with nine Irish kings and that kings in Iron Age Ireland would ritually marry her as part of their kingship ceremony.

Maeve, or characters based on her, appear in modern comics, novels, TV series, video games, and more. Some examples include *The Boys* comic book series, The Dresden Files books, the TV show *Mystic Knights of Tir Na Nog*, the mobile game *Fate/Grand Order*, and The Witcher novels.

What's Her Story?

Maeve was the daughter of Eochaid, the High King of Ireland. He gave her in marriage to Conchobar, the king of Ulster. It was not a love match, and Maeve soon left him. When she did, her father decided Maeve needed her own independent throne. So he deposed the king of Connaught, Tinni mac Conri, and made Maeve queen.

Independence suited Maeve. She ruled Connaught effectively by herself. Tinni, the previous king, had no hard feelings—he even became her friend and lover.

Later, Maeve attended an assembly of rulers at Tara, and afterward, Conchobar found her bathing in a river and raped her. In revenge, Maeve marshaled the armies of Connaught and led them to war against Ulster.

She fought courageously but ultimately had to retreat. She returned to Connaught and married a king named Eochaid who'd fought alongside her (not her dad—same name, different guy). Maeve had high standards for husbands. First, any husband of hers had to be as openhanded as she was—for she gave gifts freely, and she expected her husband to keep up with her generosity. Second, he had to be as courageous as she was, for Maeve was a fearsome warrior and she would never tolerate a husband who hid in fear while she strode boldly off to battle. And third, he couldn't be the jealous type, because Maeve's sexual appetites could never be satisfied by a single man.

Eochaid failed to live up to one of these criteria—specifically, the third one. Not long after they married, Maeve started sleeping with his bodyguard—a young, handsome man named Ailill. When Eochaid discovered this, he was enraged. He challenged Ailill to single combat—and suffered a humiliating defeat. Then Maeve married Ailill, and he took over as king of Connaught. However, it was very clear that Maeve was in charge.

Most of the time, Ailill was okay with this. But occasionally, tension arose. One day, Maeve and Ailill were lying in bed together, talking about which of them had brought more wealth to the marriage. It was a teasing, lighthearted conversation—until it wasn't.

Suddenly, they were both pulling out their belongings, from jewels and rich clothing and weapons right down to mops and buckets. It turned out they were almost exactly equal—except that Ailill had an impressive prize bull, and Maeve didn't. This could not stand.

Maeve sent messengers throughout Ireland to find another prize bull that would outshine her husband's. The only one that was a fine enough specimen was in Ulster, the kingdom of her sworn enemy. Maeve sent messengers to the bull's owner—named Daire—offering to pay him richly to borrow the bull for a year. Daire agreed and then threw a big feast to celebrate.

But at this feast, Maeve's messengers got drunk and started boasting about how if Daire hadn't agreed, they'd have taken the bull anyway. Daire, who'd had a few to drink himself, lost his temper, saying nobody took that bull anywhere without his permission—and as a matter of fact, they could just *try* to take it, because the deal was off.

As soon as Maeve received word about this, she started assembling an army to invade Ulster for the second time. The story of the ensuing war is told in the *Táin Bó Cúailnge*, or *The Cattle Raid of Cooley*. It tells of how the hero Cuchulainn fought on the Ulster side, single-handedly slowing down Maeve's army while the men of Ulster recovered from a curse that made them feel the pain of childbirth.

According to the story, Cuchulainn stalked Maeve's army, challenging her named warriors at the fords and exploding the heads of her guards, servants, and even pets with his slingstones. In retaliation, Maeve's army ravaged the land of Ulster, burned crops, rounded up livestock, and killed civilians. With her warriors terrified of Cuchulainn and threatening to desert, Maeve kept them loyal by any means necessary. As the war raged on, both Maeve and Cuchulainn stooped to acts of increasing treachery and brutality.

Finally, Maeve was forced to pull back—fighting courageously in the rear, at the center of a shield wall, guarding her army's retreat. She managed to hold the enemy off successfully—until she got her period. Maeve handed off command to one of her subordinates and stepped away to handle the situation. Legend says that her period blood dug three massive channels in the ground before she got it under control.

While she was dealing with her period, Cuchulainn himself broke through the shield wall, and finally these two intractable enemies stood face-to-face. Maeve taunted Cuchulainn to kill her, and he refused, saying he didn't kill women (although he definitely had before).

Both Maeve and Cuchulainn lived to fight another day but remained enemies. Eventually, Maeve was instrumental in bringing about Cuchulainn's death.

MARRIAGE UNDER BREHON LAW

Maeve's story offers a glimpse into an ancient Celtic culture in which women had much more freedom in marriage than was afforded by the Catholic church. Marriage in Gaelic Ireland was governed by Brehon Law—a collection of pre-Christian laws. Under Brehon Law, wives had great freedom to divorce husbands. There were different types of marriage, depending on whether the man or woman brought more property to the union. The partner who brought more wealth to the marriage had more legal standing within it. This may be why Maeve was so concerned with whether she brought more property to her marriage than Ailill—it would have established which one was the dominant partner, and possibly who had more right to rule.

MAMA HUACO

First Coya of the Inca People

PRONUNCIATION: u-AH-co

APPEARANCE: There are few descriptions of what Mama Huaco looked like, except that she was very strong and beautiful.

Overview

Mama Huaco is the founding mother of the Incan Empire in western South America, centered around the Andes Mountains. At its largest, the Incan Empire encompassed Peru, western Ecuador, Bolivia, northwest Argentina, Chile, and the southwestern tip of Colombia. She was married to Manco Cápac, the empire's founder, who was sometimes described as her brother and sometimes her son. The distinction might go back to an ancient matrilineal tradition where the right to rule passed from mother to son, or perhaps another custom that involved brother-sister marriage among Incan royals. The sources aren't clear.

Mama Huaco was a warrior and shaman who led her people to found an empire. She is considered the first Coya of the Inca people—an influential woman leader with both religious and government roles. Her parents were said to be the god of the sun and the goddess of the moon, and her

three sisters and four brothers were also part of the founding mythology of the Incan Empire.

She was a strong, fierce, and martial woman who was ferocious in battle. Along with her brother (son?) and husband Manco Cápac and her other siblings, she founded Cusco—the capital city of the Incan Empire.

However, in order to found this empire, Mama Huaco and her siblings had to colonize other people who already occupied the lands they wanted to claim. This included the Guallas and the Zañu. As such, hers is a story of conquest and war.

What's Her Story?

According to one origin story, Mama Huaco and her siblings—including Manco Cápac—were sent to earth by their father, the sun god Inti. They emerged from the cave of Paqariqtampu with a mission to found a temple of the sun in a place where their father's golden staff—entrusted to Manco Cápac—sank into the earth.

There were originally eight siblings—four men and four women. According to some versions of the story, Manco Cápac turned his three brothers to stone so he could be the undisputed leader. In some versions, he married two of his sisters, Mama Ocllo and Mama Huaco.

Among her siblings, Mama Huaco was described as exceptionally strong and skilled. She hurled two golden staffs northward to determine where her people should make their home. Both flew for miles. The first came down in Colcabamba—a mountainous region of Peru—but the ground was hard and the staff bounced off it. The second staff landed in Guayanaypata—a place known as the "navel of the world"—where it easily pierced the soft earth and sank in deep.

It's possible that the story about one staff meeting resistant ground while the other sinks in easily may be a metaphor for colonization and resistance. In some versions of the story, Mama Huaco and her party met more local resistance in some places where they tried to settle than in others.

In her most famous story, Mama Huaco and her family moved into the territory of the Guallas. They wanted to found their city there, but the Guallas were already there—and they weren't too happy about ceding their territory. So they went to war. Mama Huaco was very skilled with a slingshot. Incan armies traditionally used slingshots as long-range weapons prior to close combat. The Incan slingshot was an incredibly effective weapon, capable of hitting a target at a range of seventy meters.

Running to the front lines during the opening of battle, Mama Huaco famously shot and wounded a Guallas warrior. She then rushed to his side, cut open his chest, and breathed into it, inflating his lungs in one strong breath. This gruesome display was enough to make the Guallas flee. The Incas moved into their territory and founded their capital city, Cusco.

Mama Huaco wasn't just a terrifying warrior, however. She also taught her people to plant and harvest corn and taught the women to weave. She was known for teaching her people the skills they needed to survive in their new homeland, and she laid down the roots for the Incan civilization. Mama Huaco also had shamanic powers. She was able to make the stones and boulders speak to her and was said to be able to perform miracles.

As a leader, Mama Huaco was known for looking out for the poor in her society—and she was beloved by her people. While her husband, Manco Cápac, is generally credited with being the founding father of the Incan Empire, some traditions hold that Mama Huaco was the real power behind the throne.

Everyone respected her because of her prowess on the battlefield, her knowledge of planting and harvesting, and her shamanic gifts. Even as a Coya, she never gave up her warlike nature. She was always ready to return to the battlefield, leading her army to victory.

MAMA HUACO IN PERU TODAY

Mama Huaco is still celebrated today as a heroine in Quechua folklore. She is honored on a monument at Limacpampa Grande, a public square in the center of Cusco. Her presence can also be felt in the archaeological site at Colcampata—said to have been the palace of Manco Cápac.

But perhaps the most significant way you can feel the influence of Mama Huaco today is in humitas, bread made of sweet corn, cinnamon, and anise seeds. It is a very popular dish in Peru and is associated with Mama Huaco, as she is credited with bringing corn to her people. There are more than fifty-five varieties of Peruvian corn, many with ancient roots. The giant corn of Cusco is believed to be some of the most delicious and is known for its large kernels.

MORGAN LE FEY

Dread Sorceress of Arthurian Legend

———◆———

PRONUNCIATION: MOR-gan le FEY

AKA: Morgan le Fay ("Morgan the Fairy"), Morgen ("of the Sea"),
Morganna, Morgain, Morgane, Morgante, Morgên y Dylwythen Deg (Welsh),
Morgen an Spyrys (Cornish)

APPEARANCE: Besides being incredibly beautiful, not much is known about Morgan le Fey's appearance—perhaps because she is an enchantress and can change it at will. Morgan's beauty is a tool she uses to seduce and beguile men.

SYMBOLS:
• Avalon: Morgan is associated with the mythical island of Avalon, a magical island of learning and sorcery where King Arthur was brought when he fell on the battlefield.

———◆———

Overview

Morgan le Fey is one of the most complex and fascinating characters in the Arthurian cycle. She is sometimes the main antagonist, harassing and enchanting Arthur's knights. But she's also portrayed as a wise and powerful healer, a student of Merlin, and a friend to Arthur in his time of need.

Morgan le Fey's story was first written down in *Vita Merlini* (*The Life of Merlin*) around A.D. 1150. In some verisons of the legend she is credited as being King Arthur's supernatural half sister. She is intelligent, educated, and stunningly beautiful. In this version of the story, she is the leader of the nine women who rule Avalon—the Isle of the Fortunate, or the Isle of Apples. It's a magical land where women are trained in the magical arts, philosophy, science, healing, and many other topics.

Morgan is sexually free and chooses her own lovers. She is seen throughout the stories having affairs with different men. But it is this sexual agency, and her magical abilities, that have led to her demonization in some of the stories told to us through a Christian lens.

Morgan has a complicated relationship with her brother, King Arthur. Sometimes she helps him, and other times she tries to overthrow him and take his kingdom. The earliest sources of the Arthurian saga portray Morgan as a benevolent character. But as the stories have evolved, Morgan has taken on the role of Arthur's adversary, determined to destroy him and everything he stands for.

It's possible that these stories were crafted to vilify women who dared to step outside of the rigid patriarchal roles of medieval society and carve their own paths. Viewed in a different way, Morgan is a heroine who sees the way her brother and his knights run their kingdom, the freedoms they take from women, and the fear they have of educated women, and decides that enough is enough.

What's Her Story?

Morgan le Fey's best-known stories revolve around her rivalry with her brother, King Arthur, and his wife, Queen Guinevere. One day, while at King Arthur's court, Morgan was busy spinning thread into gold—because she was an enchantress and could do that. Queen Guinevere's nephew Guiomar laid eyes on Morgan and immediately fell in love—and the feeling was mutual. They began a passionate affair. But when Guinevere found out, she sent Guiomar away. Morgan was heartbroken. Some stories say this is why she turned against Guinevere and Arthur.

Morgan moved to the fringes of Arthur's kingdom, where she sowed discontent and harassed his knights. She tried repeatedly to seduce Lancelot, kidnapping him and keeping him captive in her castle. Lancelot refused all of Morgan's advances and instead painted murals of himself and Guinevere all over the castle. Morgan was not amused.

In one tale, Morgan and her lover Accolon plotted to overthrow Arthur. King Arthur had been incredibly successful on the battlefield because of his legendary sword, Excalibur, but also because of his little-known magical scabbard. His scabbard protected him from being harmed or wounded. So, no matter how badly someone attacked him, he always managed to walk away without a scratch.

After battle, Arthur entrusted his sword and magical scabbard to Morgan. Morgan made copies of Arthur's sword and scabbard and swapped them out, giving the real sword and scabbard to Accolon. Then Morgan, Accolon, and her knights attacked Arthur and his knights. During the battle, Arthur noticed that he was getting wounded a lot—and that shouldn't have been possible. Then he saw Accolon was in the midst of heavy battle without getting wounded at all, and he realized that Accolon had Excalibur and the magical scabbard! Arthur was able to get his scabbard back and turn the tide of the battle.

Morgan had several other unsuccessful coup attempts, including one involving a magical cloak that was supposed to catch fire and burn its wearer alive. King Arthur gave it to her unfortunate messenger and thus escaped the flames.

Eventually, Morgan gave up trying to overthrow Arthur and retired to the island of Avalon. She made peace with her brother and promised that she would be there if he needed her.

When Arthur fell in battle, Morgan was one of the women who carried his body to the barge and sailed with him to Avalon. According to some mythology, she healed him and allowed him to remain on Avalon, and he will return someday when the world has great need of him.

KING ARTHUR AND THE RISE OF THE PATRIARCHY

King Arthur's Camelot was a patriarchal kingdom where men and women had rigidly defined roles. Men were allowed to wield political power, whereas women were forced into marriage, nunneries, and the home—roles of lesser power and control in the wider world. Women like Morgan le Fey, who tried to transcend those gender roles, were depicted as villains. Women were also expected to be sexually pure—which was hypocritical, considering the liaisons and affairs Arthur and his knights had in some versions of the tales.

Morgan le Fey presided over a community where women had knowledge, power, and sexual agency. She and her women followers ruled over the blessed island of Avalon, learned about magic and the mysteries of philosophy and science, and chose their own sexual partners. They also had power outside the home—although it was magical power rather than political. Women had the ability to change shape, fly, heal, and help or hinder others. Some historians believe that Morgan le Fey represents an earlier culture that existed in the British Isles before Christianity, in which women had more power, influence, and agency.

MULAN

Valiant Chinese Heroine
Who Disguised Herself As a Man to Join the Army

PRONUNCIATION: MU-lahn

AKA: Hua Mulan

APPEARANCE: Mulan is a young fifth-century Chinese woman
who impersonated a man to join the army in her father's place.
She may be depicted as a woman or as a (disguised) male soldier.

Overview

Mulan is a pseudo-historical folk heroine in Chinese culture. Her story is known worldwide thanks to two popular Disney films. But her tale has grown and changed over the centuries and enchanted tellers and listeners since the sixth century A.D. (and probably earlier).

The story of Mulan was first written down in "The Ballad of Mulan," a folk song from the Northern Wei Dynasty of A.D. 386–535. In A.D. 429, the Wei went to war with the Rouran Khaganate, a people to the north, who were referred to as the Xiongnu in the ballad. It's believed that the story of

Mulan takes place during that time and was first written down sometime in the sixth century.

"The Ballad of Mulan" isn't long—only thirty-one couplets—but it has captured imaginations for more than a thousand years. The story has been adapted across many different mediums, including operas, plays, novels, films, and countless pieces of artwork.

What's Her Story?

"The Ballad of Mulan" opens with Mulan sitting at her loom and lamenting the fact that her aging father has been conscripted into the army. He is too old to have much of a chance of surviving a long campaign, and her younger brother is too young to serve for him. So Mulan does the unthinkable: She decides to go to war in her father's place.

She goes to four different markets to buy the things she'll need for war—a horse, a saddle and stirrups, a bridle and reins, and a long whip. She visits many different shops to keep her purchases a secret and to avoid anyone figuring out what she's up to. What she is about to do is dangerous and transgressive: defy the codified gender roles and go off to war as a man.

The next day, Mulan bids her family farewell and rides to the Black Mountain by the Yellow River, where she meets up with the rest of the soldiers and begins a ten- or twelve-year campaign (depending on the translation). She fights in more than a hundred battles, forming strong bonds with other soldiers, who never suspect that she is not a man.

After the war ends, the emperor calls together all the veterans to shower the highest-ranking ones with praise and honors. He is so impressed with Mulan that he offers her a chance to stay at the palace and become his adviser, or *shàng shū láng*—a very high-ranking position in the government. But Mulan is tired of pretending to be someone she's not. She asks the emperor for a fast horse so that she may return home to her family. Her simple request is granted.

THE NORTHERN WEI DYNASTY

"The Ballad of Mulan" doesn't give a concrete historical setting, but it is attributed to the Northern Wei Dynasty because of geographical and cultural references. For instance, the Black Mountain and the Yellow River were both landmarks within this kingdom. Another interesting reference in the poem is that the emperor in the ballad is referred to as a khan. This is a ruling title that the Rouran Khaganate, the people the Wei were at war with, also used. Both were nomadic horse archers from the northern Eurasian steppe, and they were thought to be distantly related.

The Northern Wei Dynasty was founded by the Tuoba, a clan of the Xianbei people. The Xianbei were skilled horseback riders and archers, and both women and men fought. They were nomadic until they united and settled in northern China, when they changed their name to Wei and founded their kingdom in an area that is still considered China's traditional heartland. But women going to war may not have been that unusual just a few generations prior to Mulan's time.

The emperors of the Northern Wei established what would become the enduring governing institutions of imperial China—including the office of *shàng shū láng*. This was the highest ministerial position in the government and was granted to someone with experience in combat as well as skill in reading and writing. In other words, this role was only given to someone who excelled at battle, strategy, and literacy. It was not a role traditionally open to women, with the exception of Mulan.

Some of Mulan's friends from the army come home with her. And when they arrive, the town throws a party to celebrate them. Mulan prepares for the party by washing, changing out of her armor, donning makeup, combing her hair, and putting on the traditional clothing of a fifth-century Chinese woman.

When she leaves the house, all the other soldiers she served with are shocked to see that she's a woman. They cannot believe that they fought with her for so long and never realized.

Mulan explains that you can tell a male and female rabbit apart when they are sitting side by side—the male's front paws are a little bigger and the female has a squint. But when the two rabbits are running together, it would be impossible to tell the difference. This metaphor is Mulan's way of telling the soldiers that during battle, when she fought side by side with these men, it would have been impossible to tell that she was a woman—and maybe the point is that, in wartime, it doesn't matter anyway.

SCHEHERAZADE

Spellbinding Storyteller of
One Thousand and One Nights

PRONUNCIATION: she-HE-ra-zad

AKA: Shahrazad, Čehrāzād; may be derived from a name in
Middle Persian that means "Noble Lineage"

APPEARANCE: Scheherazade was said to be beautiful, but most descriptions of her
emphasize her nonphysical qualities: that she was intelligent, well read,
highly educated, and a very talented storyteller.

Overview

Scheherazade is the heroine of *One Thousand and One Nights*, a collection of Middle Eastern and Indian folktales first compiled during the Islamic Golden Age. There are many iconic stories in *One Thousand and One Nights* that are familiar to audiences worldwide—including "Aladdin," "Ali Baba and the Forty Thieves," "The Seven Voyages of Sinbad the Sailor," and many more.

Scheherazade's story acts as a framing device for the rest of the tales in the collection. She's married to a king who has a nasty habit of killing his wives every morning so they don't have time to betray him. Every night,

Scheherazade tells him a riveting tale, keeping him on the edge of his seat and ending the story on a cliff hanger. And every morning, he spares her life for one more night so he can hear the end of her tale.

Scheherazade is, above all, a consummate storyteller, constantly saving her own life and eventually calming the king's bloodlust through the power of a compelling tale. It's no surprise that her own story has fascinated generations and inspired centuries of novels, plays, poetry, films, and more.

What's Her Story?

The king of this story was Shahryar, the ruler of a Sassanid Empire so vast that it stretched all the way to India and past the Ganges River, into China. He was fictional, and although the Sassanid Empire was real, the bounds of it in this story are probably fictional as well. One day, King Shahryar discovered that his queen was cheating on him. He was so distraught that he had her executed, and then he went berserk with grief and started to make even more questionable choices.

Shahryar had no heir, and he knew that he would have to marry again soon. But he believed that all women were wicked at their core, and it was only a matter of time before they would betray him as his wife did. So he married someone new every day, spent one night with her, and then had her beheaded the next morning before she could cheat on him. He did this over and over for many days. This caused chaos both in Shahryar's realm and abroad. His people rebelled and his allies turned against him. Families with daughters of marriageable age fled the country.

Shahryar's vizier, tasked with both finding brides for him and overseeing their executions, even begged his own two daughters to flee. Both refused to leave. His elder daughter, Scheherazade, took things one step further by volunteering to be the next bride. She told her father she had a plan that would put a stop to the killings.

The vizier pleaded with Scheherazade to give up her dangerous plan. But Scheherazade was insistent. So the vizier went to Shahryar and told him that there were no suitable women left for him to marry, except one—and then offered him his own daughter.

Scheherazade was very beautiful, not to mention smart, well read, highly educated, and a sparkling conversationalist. Just as the vizier expected, the king accepted immediately. On their wedding night, Scheherazade told him that she knew she was scheduled for execution in the morning and asked his permission to send for her younger sister to say goodbye.

Shahryar, who had taken rather a liking to Scheherazade (despite the fact that he really didn't like women in general), agreed. So Scheherazade sent for her sister, Dunyazad. She told her sister a story, spinning the tale throughout the night. Shahryar stayed awake and listened, utterly riveted by Scheherazade's incredible storytelling.

As dawn broke, Scheherazade ended her story at a carefully chosen spot, leaving key plot points unresolved. The king agreed to let her live one more night so that he could hear the end of that story. Scheherazade continued to weave her tales for the king, always ending on a cliff-hanger that kept him wanting more.

Finally, after a thousand and one nights of this, Shahryar realized that he had fallen in love with her and asked her to become his queen—and the cycle of violence was broken.

THE HISTORY OF
ONE THOUSAND AND ONE NIGHTS

One Thousand and One Nights (also known as *The Arabian Nights* in English translations) is a group of stories that were compiled over hundreds of years. The origins of the collection—and its original compiler—are mysterious and the subject of much debate. Some of the tales are much older than the compilation as a whole and are influenced by Sanskrit, Indian, Persian, Buddhist, Thai, Tamil, Egyptian, and many other traditions and sources. Some scholars believe that a core of older Persian and Indian tales were perhaps first translated into Arabic during the eighth century A.D. Over the centuries, new stories were added from Iraq, Syria, Egypt, and other places, growing the collection into the longer version we know today.

SKY WOMAN

The First Woman of Huron and Iroquois Mythology

AKA: Grandmother Moon, the Woman Who Fell from the Sky,
Ataensic, Atahensic, Ataentsi

APPEARANCE: Sky Woman is described as a beautiful Native American woman.
Sometimes she is depicted as pregnant.

Overview

Sky Woman's story is an ever-evolving oral tradition that varies from community to community. Her story originates with the Iroquois and Huron peoples but can also be found among other Indigenous peoples in North America.

The story begins long before the creation of our world, on the floating island that lay above the earth, in the sky. On this island, people never grew old and never experienced sadness or hunger. In the center of this island grew a tree that gave off all the light that the people needed to live by. The sun hadn't been created yet, and so this tree was vital for the people. Everything was a virtual paradise, until one day, when a woman, Sky Woman, became pregnant with twins.

What's Her Story?

In some versions of the story, when Sky Woman told her husband that she would be having twins, he was so angry that he uprooted the tree and pushed his wife through the hole in the sky. In other versions, the tree broke and left a hole in the sky. Overwhelmed with curiosity, Sky Woman peeked down into the hole and saw the vast oceans and waves below in another world. She was so transfixed that she slipped and fell through.

As she fell, waterfowl flew to help slow her descent. When she landed, a turtle rose from the sea and offered his back for Sky Woman to rest on—because, at this point, the world was covered in an all-encompassing ocean.

Sky Woman created land with the help of the creatures around her. In some versions of the story, a toad or muskrat dove down to the bottom of the sea and brought up some mud. The birds and Sky Woman spread the mud across the turtle's back, and the land grew and grew until it became the size of the continent of North America.

Once the land was created, Sky Woman sprinkled dust into the air and made the stars, moon, and sun. She brought down helpful plants from the realm of the sky, which she grew on the turtle's back.

Eventually, Sky Woman gave birth to twin boys—Sapling and Flint. They grew up quickly, and as they grew, they continued the work of expanding the world their mother had created on the turtle's back. Sapling was kind and gentle and created things that reflected this—edible plants, fish without bones, rivers that flowed in two directions, and many other things that would help people live lives without suffering.

But his brother, Flint, was the opposite. Flint was aggressive and confrontational, and he created fish with bones, rivers that only went one way, mountains, caverns, thorns on berry bushes, and the season of winter.

But Sapling infused winter with life and purpose, so that the season would move on rather than stay in one place. In this way, winter gave way to spring and summer, thus creating the seasons.

The brothers were two sides of the same coin. One day, they decided to have a fight for dominance. Sapling and Flint battled, and Sapling won. He drove Flint deep underground. (You can sometimes still feel Flint's anger in the shaking and eruptions of volcanoes.)

When Sky Woman died, Sapling buried her body with a seed. From her grave, the first corn plant grew, nourished by Sky Woman's body. The corn became an important crop that fed all of her descendants.

Sky Woman's story is one of birth, fertility, and creation. It particularly highlights a respect and love for the animal world and shows how crucial animals are in helping humanity survive and making the world livable.

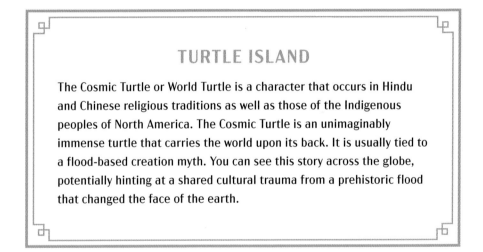

TURTLE ISLAND

The Cosmic Turtle or World Turtle is a character that occurs in Hindu and Chinese religious traditions as well as those of the Indigenous peoples of North America. The Cosmic Turtle is an unimaginably immense turtle that carries the world upon its back. It is usually tied to a flood-based creation myth. You can see this story across the globe, potentially hinting at a shared cultural trauma from a prehistoric flood that changed the face of the earth.

Turtle Island is a name sometimes used for the earth—or the continent of North America—by Indigenous peoples in the United States and Canada. It is becoming more and more common for people in North America to begin gatherings and proceedings with a spoken acknowledgment of Indigenous peoples' territories and the Turtle Island on which these events take place.

SPLINTER FOOT GIRL

Arapaho Star Maiden

AKA: Foot Stuck Child, Heseihteesiisoo, Häsixtäciisan, Hasixtaciisan

APPEARANCE: Splinter Foot Girl is described as a beautiful, young Native American girl.

SYMBOLS:
• The Pleiades: She and her fathers are said to have formed this constellation, making up the seven stars.

Overview

Splinter Foot Girl is central to the traditions of the Arapaho people. Her story is one of struggle and transformation. Prior to European colonization, the Arapaho were farmers who harvested crops and hunted buffalo on the Great Plains. However, due to the aggressive expansion of Europeans, they were forced farther westward and into a lifestyle that involved moving around frequently to hunt buffalo. They began living in homes of buffalo hides that could be quickly assembled and disassembled. They were able to pack up their belongings and move their entire communities within hours if necessary.

Many people lived in smaller groups and went out together as hunting parties. And that is where Splinter Foot Girl's story begins. Hers is a story of a girl traveling to the ends of the earth to be free of relentless suitors. Between the lines of this story, you can see the tale of a people driven to the ends of the continent by the oppression and greed of European settlers.

What's Her Story?

Splinter Foot Girl's story begins, as you might imagine, with a splinter.

A large group of people were out hunting. Many of them grew tired and went home, but seven young men decided to journey on. When one of their party grew too tired to go any farther, they made camp.

One day, while out hunting, one young man scraped his leg on a thorny bush. It swelled up, and he had to stop hunting for days. Then the wound on his leg burst open, and out came a baby girl. The men called her Splinter Foot Girl because she had been born from the splinter in the man's leg.

The men grew to love the girl. They took turns looking after her and raised her as their daughter. They taught her to hunt and survive. Rumors of Splinter Foot Girl's beauty spread across the Plains, and soon suitors began to ask for her hand in marriage. First came Bone Bull. He sent a variety of birds to the young men to plead his case for marrying the girl. At first the men rejected Bone Bull's proposals. Splinter Foot Girl was too young, and they didn't want to let her go. But Bone Bull became more and more insistent, until finally the fathers agreed.

The only one happy about this marriage was Bone Bull. Splinter Foot Girl was miserable and so were her fathers. So the fathers made a plan to bring her home.

They managed to get the support of local animals, including flies, birds, moles, and badgers. Finally, a mole and a badger worked under the cover of darkness, digging a hole that would allow Splinter Foot Girl to escape her husband. Splinter Foot Girl crawled through the hole and was reunited with her fathers. But they knew that they could not celebrate for too long, because Bone Bull would come looking for his wife. So they ran, looking for a place to hide, but whenever they stopped, the land refused to shelter them because of its fear of Bone Bull.

Finally, they reached a cottonwood tree. The tree told Splinter Foot Girl and her fathers to climb up high into its branches and rest. It would not allow Bone Bull to harm them.

Eventually, Bone Bull arrived at the foot of the tree, looking for his wife. But the tree refused to give up the girl. Bone Bull bellowed in rage and charged the tree, which proved to be a terrible idea. He got his horns stuck in the wood, and one of Splinter Foot Girl's fathers shot and killed him, putting an end to that marriage.

But word soon got out that Splinter Foot Girl was now single, and Merciless-Man, who was a rock, was the next to propose marriage. The fathers were warned that Merciless-Man was cruel to his wives. But the rock was powerful, and in the end, they decided to have Splinter Foot Girl marry the rock and then escape him—with a little help from Badger and Mole.

So Splinter Foot Girl married the rock, and once again, Badger and Mole dug a hole. But this time, the hole was for the rock. When Merciless-Man returned from his daily work, Splinter Foot Girl tricked him into rolling into the hole. Then she absconded with Badger and Mole and returned to her fathers.

They ran all night, but the rock soon rolled out of his hole and caught up with them. Seeing no other escape, Splinter Foot Girl took a ball she'd been carrying and kicked it into the sky, turning one of her fathers into a star as she did and propelling him into the sky with the ball. One by one, she turned her fathers into stars as she kicked the ball into the sky. Finally, it was her turn, and she kicked the ball one final time, joining her fathers in the sky and forming the constellation Pleiades.

Splinter Foot Girl finally made a place for herself and her fathers to be safe and free. To this day, she and her fathers live in the sky in a tent made of stars.

THE PLEIADES AROUND THE WORLD

Pleiades is the scientific name of the constellation of stars that is visible almost everywhere on earth. *Pleiades* means "sail" in Greek. This constellation's arrival in the northern hemisphere usually heralds the coming of winter. Because the Pleiades is so ubiquitous, the constellation features in folklore, mythology, and religious traditions around the globe. It also served as an important point in the planting cycle for many agricultural societies. For example:

- In the Mediterranean, the arrival of the Pleiades in the morning sky before sunrise meant it was the navigation season, when it was safe to sail.
- In Europe, the Pleiades' culmination—when it reaches the highest point in the sky—coincided with a Druid festival at the end of autumn. It was believed that this was when the veil between the worlds was at its thinnest—giving rise to mythology surrounding Halloween and Samhain, during which ghosts and supernatural beings cross over into the mortal realm.
- The Zuni of New Mexico marked the arrival of the Pleiades as a sign that it was time to begin planting.

All across the globe, the Pleiades have come to mean something different, inspiring stories and legends. Perhaps none is as fascinating as the story of Splinter Foot Girl.

THÁKANE

Basotho Dragon Slayer and Monster Hunter

PRONUNCIATION: THA-ka-neh

SYMBOLS:

• Crocodiles: Thákane is famous for slaying the *nanabolele*,
a mythological crocodile-like dragon.

Overview

Thákane is a legendary princess of the Basotho in southern Africa. Her mother died in childbirth, and her father died when she was an adult. After her father's death, Thákane was left caring for her two bratty little brothers.

She had to play the roles of both mother and father to the boys, and it was her responsibility to prepare them to rule someday. (As a woman, Thákane couldn't rule in her own right.) Part of preparing her brothers to rule meant making sure they got to school. The boys, predictably, were not appreciative of her efforts. They demanded that Thákane go to great lengths to provide them with the privileges and benefits that their father would have.

Thákane did this, possibly out of a sense of duty toward her father—or out of sheer determination to prove anyone wrong who thought she couldn't do it. This led her to do some truly badass acts of monster slaying.

In modern popular culture, Thákane has been featured in *Rejected Princesses* and in an episode of the *Myths and Legends* podcast.

What's Her Story?

When Thákane's father died, her brothers were next in line to serve as chieftains, and part of preparing for that involved undergoing training as warriors. Thákane spent months dragging her brothers out of bed and marching them up into the mountains for warrior school. Without their sister, the boys would have dropped out ages before. But because of Thákane's tireless efforts, they eventually graduated.

At their graduation ceremony, their father was supposed to present them each with armor and a shield made out of the skin of a fearsome beast he had killed himself. Since their father was dead, Thákane did this for him, slaying a lion herself and crafting armor and shields from its skin.

But the boys did not appreciate her efforts. They complained that *everyone* got lion shields and armor, and as the sons of a chieftain, they deserved something better. They demanded gifts made from an even scarier beast than a lion. Maybe even a *nanabolele*.

A *nanabolele* is a water dragon in Basotho legend—kind of like a super-sized glow-in-the-dark crocodile that emits a crimson cloud of smoke. They're virtually indestructible, and nobody believed that Thákane could slay one. Maybe just to prove everyone wrong, Thákane got a band of friends together and went off to find some *nanabolele*.

They went down to the river, where they threw chunks of ox meat into the water as bait. Thákane sang an insulting song daring the *nanabolele* to come out and fight her. All that emerged were some eels, who told them they were hunting in the wrong place and to keep going up the river.

So Thákane and her friends kept going, tossing meat into the river and singing taunting songs. Along the way, frogs and other water denizens would helpfully tell them to keep on; they were getting close.

Finally, an old woman emerged from the water. She beckoned the group to follow her into the river, to where an entire second river existed under the water. Beside it was a village, which was deserted because the *nanabolele* had killed everyone who lived there (except the old woman, who was too tough to eat). They'd enslaved her instead, and she was sick of cooking and cleaning for them.

So the old woman hid Thákane and her friends while they waited for the *nanabolele* to return. Eventually, they did, and although they smelled the hiding humans, they couldn't find them. (They weren't that bright.) After a while, they quit looking and fell asleep. And while they slept, Thákane walked up to the largest, scariest one, killed it, and skinned it.

Then they had to flee—because dawn was coming, and when the other *nanabolele* woke, they were going to be out for vengeance. But the old lady first gave Thákane a magical stone that would protect them if they were followed.

Thákane thanked the old woman, and then she and her friends emerged from the river and ran. As soon as dawn broke, a great plume of crimson smoke rose up on the horizon. The *nanabolele* were on their trail, and they were *mad*. So Thákane threw down the stone the old woman had given her. Immediately, up sprouted a mountain so huge that the *nanabolele* could not follow.

This happened several times, and each time Thákane threw down the stone and the *nanabolele* tried and failed to scale the mountain. Finally, when they arrived back at their village, Thákane set her dogs on the *nanabolele* and ran them off for good.

Then Thákane had the skins she'd collected made into shields and armor for her brothers. They were very pleased, strutting around in their new clothes.

In some versions of the story, her brothers were so happy that they gave her a hundred cattle, making her a wealthy woman in her own right, if not a chieftain. In others, she married the son of a chieftain from a neighboring village and became a queen.

THÁKANE'S LOVE INTEREST: PRINCE MASILO

In one version of the story, Thákane fell in love as part of her quest. Her love interest was Prince Masilo. He was the son of a chieftain in a neighboring village, and when he heard that Thákane was looking for brave warriors to join in her quest to get a *nanabolele* skin, he wanted to join the expedition for the honor of his family.

He was super impressed with this brave warrior woman who was looking to go kill dragons. His father forbade him to go, however, because it was dangerous and he might get killed. But Masilo snuck off and joined Thákane's entourage anyway.

The more he got to know her and saw her courage in action, the more impressed he was. Thákane thought he was kind of cute—but she was busy killing monsters, so she wasn't exactly ready for something serious. But after they brought the skins back to her village, she agreed to marry him.

TRIỆU THỊ TRINH

Elephant-Riding Rebel General of Ancient Vietnam

PRONUNCIATION: cheu ti chin

AKA: Lady Triệu, Bà Triệu, Triệu Thị Chin

APPEARANCE: Triệu Thị Trinh was said to be 9 feet tall, with 3-foot-long breasts that she threw over her shoulder when she rode her elephant into battle. According to legend, she was so beautiful that she could shake a man down to his soul.

SYMBOLS:

• **Elephants:** Triệu Thị Trinh was famous for riding a war elephant.

Overview

Triệu Thị Trinh is a war leader and resistance fighter from third-century Vietnam. She was most likely a real historical figure, although some details about her—such as that she was 9 feet tall—show that she achieved a legendary reputation, either during her lifetime or after her death. Many of the most incredible details about her life—for instance, that she rode a war elephant into battle and fought more than thirty battles before the age of twenty-one—may well have been true.

During Triệu Thị Trinh's lifetime, Vietnam was occupied by the Eastern Wu Dynasty of China. The Eastern Wu emperor imposed heavy taxes and oppressive laws, working to assimilate the proud, independent Vietnamese people into Chinese culture. Prior to that, Vietnam had been occupied by the Han Dynasty of China; other rebellions rose up over the centuries, and these were violently stamped out.

In Vietnam today, Triệu Thị Trinh is considered a national heroine. Streets and schools are named for her, and children learn about her in school. She is less well known outside Vietnam; in modern popular culture, she is featured in the video games *Civilization VI* and *Total War: Three Kingdoms*.

What's Her Story?

Triệu Thị Trinh's parents died when she was very young, and she was raised in the household of her older brother.

During this time, Vietnam was under occupation by the Eastern Wu Dynasty of China. In A.D. 226, the Eastern Wu emperor purged the Vietnamese ruling family, who had been allowed to rule at least nominally up until then. When Vietnamese people rose up in protest, the Chinese killed thousands.

Triệu Thị Trinh and her brother, Triệu Quốc Đạt, fled to the mountains, where they recruited a corps of warriors and trained them to fight the Chinese. Triệu Thị Trinh was nineteen years old at the time, and when her brother tried to convince her to get married instead, she openly defied him. She declared that she wanted to "brave the tempest, kill sharks in the sea, fight off the oppressors, restore our country to our people, break the bonds of slavery—and never bow down and be a concubine to any man."

Both Triệu Thị Trinh and Triệu Quốc Đạt were very dedicated to the rebel cause, but some versions say that Triệu Quốc Đạt's wife tried to inform on them to the Chinese. Triệu Thị Trinh killed her brother's wife herself, in order to send a strong message to their troops—this is what happens to traitors. Other versions suggest that the sister-in-law was abusive, and Triệu Thị Trinh killed her in an argument and then fled to the mountains to begin raising her army.

Triệu Quốc Đạt died during the war effort, and Triệu Thị Trinh assumed full control of the rebel army. She led her war band to take on the Chinese and fought bravely in more than thirty battles before she turned twenty-one. She was famous for riding an elephant into battle, and she could always be found on the front lines where the fighting was fiercest.

In some versions of the tale, Triệu Thị Trinh's elephant was said to be a one-tusked albino elephant who had been wreaking havoc in local communities. Nobody—not the people whose property it destroyed, and not the hunters who wanted its valuable tusks—could get near the elephant. Triệu Thị Trinh managed to befriend and tame it, and from then on it became her devoted companion in battle.

She quickly began to build a legendary reputation. It was said that she was over 9 feet tall, with a voice as loud as a bell, and breasts 3 feet long, which she threw over her shoulders when she rode her elephant. (She could have benefited from a supportive sports bra.)

She also had a reputation for wearing golden armor, which was probably closer to the truth (because how would she throw her breasts over her shoulder while wearing a breastplate?). War leaders in ancient times often wore flashy armor so they could be seen easily by their soldiers. Riding atop her elephant in bright golden armor, Triệu Thị Trinh would have been very visible. Of course, that would also have made her a target to the other side—but she took the risk as a bold, courageous, and confident warrior.

The Chinese, however, were determined to put down Triệu Thị Trinh's rebellion. In A.D. 248, the emperor sent all the troops he could spare to Vietnam. He also sent agents to bribe people in Triệu Thị Trinh's army to inform on her and turn against her.

Eventually, despite her courage and skill in battle, Triệu Thị Trinh was overcome. Some legends say she was killed in battle, others that she fled the battlefield after her final defeat and later died by suicide. But her legend lived on, inspiring generations of Vietnamese people.

THE TRƯNG SISTERS

Triệu Thị Trinh wasn't the only Vietnamese woman who led warriors in battle against Chinese occupiers. Almost two hundred years before her time, in A.D. 40, the Trưng sisters bravely took on the Han emperor. Their names were Trưng Trắc (the older sister) and Trưng Nhị (the younger). Trưng Trắc's husband, a member of the local aristocracy, led a rebellion against the Han governor of the region—a man with a reputation for brutality—and was captured and beheaded. Trưng Trắc and Trưng Nhị immediately pulled together a much larger army to avenge his death. They were incredibly successful at first, driving Chinese forces out of much of Vietnam—some accounts say they also rode elephants into battle—and Trưng Trắc became Vietnam's first queen. Their victory didn't last, however. Fighting continued, and by A.D. 43, the Han Dynasty had won back most of Vietnam. The Trưng sisters may have been captured and beheaded, or possibly they drowned themselves in a river to escape capture.

URDUJA

Filipina Warrior Princess, Diplomat, and Stateswoman

———◆———

PRONUNCIATION: Ur-DU-ha

APPEARANCE: She is described as being tall and beautiful with golden-bronze skin, long dark hair, and dark brown eyes. She is usually dressed in gold. She is a warrior, skilled with the sword and often depicted on horseback.

———◆———

Overview

Urduja is a legendary warrior princess from the Philippines. While her story may have been based on a real person, it is likely that Urduja is a folk heroine whose legend has grown over the centuries.

Urduja was a princess of Tawalisi, a kingdom in Southeast Asia believed to have been located in what is now the region of Pangasinan in the Philippines. Her legend dates to the fourteenth century, prior to European colonization.

She personally led her army into battle, but she was also a skilled diplomat and stateswoman and managed to keep her country together during the chaotic fourteenth century.

Today, Urduja is considered a national heroine in the Philippines. There are statues of her and schools named after her, and in 2008 an animated movie about her life, called *Urduja*, was released. There is also an asteroid, 5749 Urduja, named in her honor.

What's Her Story?

Urduja appears in the writings of the Moroccan author and traveler Ibn Battuta, who described her as a young, highly intelligent, and beautiful princess of Tawalisi who led her people into battle and fought at their side.

As the Shri-Visayan Empire rose to power in the sixth through fourteenth centuries, Urduja's kingdom faced almost-constant war. As princess, Urduja knew her country was in crisis: Too many men had been killed in battle, and soon it would not be able to defend itself. With the population of fighting-age men so depleted, Urduja needed to find a way to strengthen her army and protect her people. So she had the women of her country trained in the art of warfare. They became excellent horsewomen, soldiers, and sword fighters, protecting their country from outside aggressors and consistently winning battles. They made Tawalisi a place to be revered and respected.

Urduja trained a retinue of highly skilled warrior women called the Kinalakian or Kalakian. These women were physically very strong and were more than a match for any man they met on the battlefield.

When the time came for Urduja to marry, she swore she would never marry anyone who couldn't beat her in a duel; some versions of the story say it was a wrestling match. Further, she would only marry someone who was wiser, stronger, and smarter than her.

In her entire life, she never found a match. She remained very happily single.

In addition to her other roles and talents, Urduja was also a stateswoman who spoke many languages and dialects. She was interested in travelers from all over the world, but particularly India. She famously opened her court to travelers and welcomed them into her kingdom. For example, the explorer and author Ibn Battuta wrote of visiting her court in the fourteenth century. He described the many valuable gifts she gave him, including salted mangoes, ginger, pepper, and lemons, as well as rich robes, buffaloes, and a supply of rice for his journey.

She was knowledgeable in many different cultures and customs and took pride in showing off this knowledge to her visitors. Essentially, she used this as a chance to prove that women knew just as much as male rulers and ruled just as efficiently, if not more so.

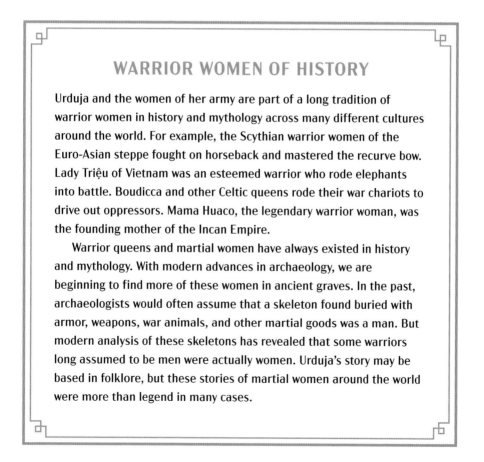

WARRIOR WOMEN OF HISTORY

Urduja and the women of her army are part of a long tradition of warrior women in history and mythology across many different cultures around the world. For example, the Scythian warrior women of the Euro-Asian steppe fought on horseback and mastered the recurve bow. Lady Triệu of Vietnam was an esteemed warrior who rode elephants into battle. Boudicca and other Celtic queens rode their war chariots to drive out oppressors. Mama Huaco, the legendary warrior woman, was the founding mother of the Incan Empire.

Warrior queens and martial women have always existed in history and mythology. With modern advances in archaeology, we are beginning to find more of these women in ancient graves. In the past, archaeologists would often assume that a skeleton found buried with armor, weapons, war animals, and other martial goods was a man. But modern analysis of these skeletons has revealed that some warriors long assumed to be men were actually women. Urduja's story may be based in folklore, but these stories of martial women around the world were more than legend in many cases.

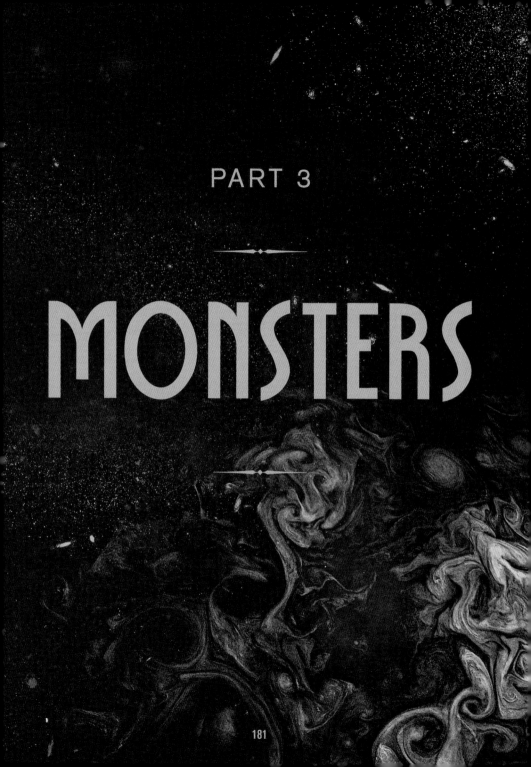

PART 3

MONSTERS

AICHA KANDICHA

Camel-Hoofed Seductress of Moroccan Legend

PRONUNCIATION: a-EE-sha con-DEE-sha

AKA: Aicha Qandicha, Kharaja, Aisha Kandisha

APPEARANCE: Aicha Kandicha is a beautiful young Moroccan woman from the waist up. From the waist down, she has the legs of a camel or goat. She can also shape-shift, taking on the appearance of her victim's wife or lover.

SYMBOLS:

- **Water:** Aicha Kandicha is always tied to a specific body of water.

Overview

Aicha Kandicha is a famous figure in Moroccan folklore: a spirit who lures men to their deaths or madness. Sometimes she is considered to be a djinn, which is a supernatural being or spirit from pre-Islamic Arabic mythology (you can read more about them in the El Naddāha entry later in this part). She is said to live near water sources—rivers, streams, wells, or the sea—where she hunts and waits for her prey, mostly young men.

Today, Aicha Kandicha has become a kind of urban legend. Parents sometimes use the fear of her to encourage good behavior in their children, and there are also stories of men's frightening encounters with her. But the truth of her legend may be rooted in a different type of horror: colonialism.

In modern times, you can find mentions of her in many Moroccan songs, books, and films. A horror film about Aicha Kandicha, called *Kandisha*, was released in France in 2020.

What's Her Story?

Aicha Kandicha is known for luring young men to their deaths. She waits by a body of water, and when a young man comes upon her, she seduces him—then either possesses him and drives him to madness or kills him. Sometimes she toys with her victims before killing them.

She is said to be extremely beautiful—the perfect predator's camouflage, ideal for luring and beguiling her victims. She is also said to be able to take the form of her victims' wives and lovers and trick them into falling under her power. Despite her beauty, Aicha Kandicha is described as having the legs of a camel—or sometimes a goat or donkey, depending on the version. Often, spotting her unusual legs can be the difference between life or death for her victims.

Aicha Kandicha is frequently associated with a specific body of water, which changes depending on the region of Morocco. In some regions, it's the sea; in others, she is tied to a particular river; in some areas, she is said to make her home in a well or drainage canal.

Modern urban legends depict people encountering Aicha Kandicha if they stray too close to the body of water where she lives. Those walking alone at night are particularly vulnerable, but having a car won't necessarily protect you. Some stories tell of her waiting alone by the side of the road. Her victim spots her and chivalrously offers her a ride—sometimes the victim is a taxi driver—only to see her transform into something monstrous in the car.

In the urban legends, those who live to tell the tale tend to notice her animal legs before she can get close enough to bewitch them. Sometimes, men who escape return later to the scene of the encounter and see her hoofprints in the dirt.

Aicha Kandicha's legend has grown to include some unique weaknesses and powers. According to some versions of her tale, she has a fear of steel knives and needles. In other versions, she is able to cause miscarriage in any pregnant woman who lays eyes on her. Still other versions give her the power to possess people and make them bray or bark.

IS AICHA KANDICHA A REBEL COUNTESS?

The story of Aicha Kandicha may have its roots in the colonization of Morocco. This region of North Africa has always been sought-after. For example, the Phoenicians colonized its coastline as early as the eighth century B.C., the Portuguese occupied Morocco in the 1400s, and the French occupied it in the twentieth century. Because the area is so desired, there have been many wars and conflicts over the years.

Aicha Kandicha might be based on a real fifteenth-century countess from El Jadida, a major port city in Morocco. During this time, Morocco was occupied by the Portuguese. This countess was a resistance fighter known for her exceptional beauty, cunning, and intelligence. According to the story, she would lure Portuguese soldiers out at night for a rendezvous on a deserted beach—where they would be slaughtered by Moroccan freedom fighters. This theory about the origins of Aicha Kandicha's legend combines some of the most lurid elements of mythology: a beautiful woman, a cunning plan to entrap men and lure them to their deaths, and a setting that involved the sea or bodies of water.

AL KARISI

Liver-Stealing Demoness of Childbirth

PRONUNCIATION: AL kar-ISS-ee

AKA: Alk (Kurdish and Armenian), Al (Iranian),
Hāl or Xāl (Afghan and Tajik), Halmasti (Dardic)

APPEARANCE: Al Karisi may appear as an old woman or
monster dressed in red. Descriptions vary across cultures.

SYMBOLS:
• The color red: Al Karisi's name in Turkish means
"Red Woman" or "Scarlet Woman."
• Fire: In some traditions, Al Karisi is linked to fire.

Overview

Versions of Al Karisi are found across a broad territory—from the Caucasus to the Middle East and central Asia. Varieties of her legend occur in the folklore of Afghanistan, Iran, Mongolia, Tajikistan, Turkey, and Bosnia and Herzegovina, as well as in Kurdish and Dardic communities, among many others.

Al Karisi is a demoness of childbirth. While some traditions hold that she can be both a man and a woman, she is usually depicted as a woman. In Iranian folklore, she appears as a thin old woman with a nose of clay and a face flushed red. Other traditions describe her as a creature with fangs, tangled hair, teeth of iron, claws of copper, and the tusks of a wild boar. She may have sagging breasts or a habit of throwing one breast over a shoulder. She may also be a shape-shifter, appearing as a bird, cat, dog, or someone her victim knows.

She has names in many different languages. She is called Al Karisi in Turkish folklore; the name means "Red Woman" or "Scarlet Woman." This is related to the red dress she wears, but it may also be linked to her association with fire.

What's Her Story?

Al Karisi has a frightening reputation for causing problems with childbirth. According to some traditions, she causes miscarriages and can also kill or carry away babies shortly after birth. She also targets new mothers. Depending on the folklore, Al Karisi may stalk a pregnant victim for some time but usually waits until after childbirth to attack. Her usual method is to steal the victim's internal organs—often the liver. She is sometimes depicted as carrying a bag or sack with which to carry off the victim's organs.

Childbirth has always been a dangerous time for women and babies across cultures, both in ancient times and in many places today. Al Karisi's behavior may be associated with unexplained deaths among infants and new mothers in the premodern world. She was said to target babies in the first forty days after childbirth, and mythology about her may have been connected to sudden infant death syndrome (SIDS) and other unexplained deaths of infants.

Some versions of the tale say that she has a hypnotic gaze that can render her victims immobile, awake but unable to move as Al Karisi harvests their organs. This may connect her with the phenomenon of sleep paralysis.

Despite the terrible nature of her attacks, Al Karisi's crime scenes are generally described to be bloodless. No wounds are found on the victim's body, and little evidence can be seen of her presence except the victim's death—either suddenly or, in some traditions, over time due to a wasting sickness.

Because of this, Al Karisi may have also been used as a scapegoat for unexplained illness or deaths of mothers after childbirth. Perhaps stories of her were used as a way to explain conditions such as preeclampsia, which affects the liver and kidneys and can, in some rare instances, occur suddenly even after childbirth.

Stories of Al Karisi and her counterparts are also linked to stories of Lilith, the original wife of Adam in other mythologies, and another childbirth demoness whose story you'll find later in this part. According to some tellings, it was Al Karisi, not Lilith, who was the original wife of Adam. But because Adam was made of earth and Al Karisi was made of fire, the two did not get along—their natures were too different. Al Karisi was too wild and passionate for Adam to control.

So Al Karisi was replaced with Eve, and there was enmity between the two women from then on. Like Lilith's story, this legend may be a way to explain why Al Karisi targets new mothers and the children of Eve.

HOW TO WARD OFF AL KARISI

Al Karisi can be a terrifying demoness for new mothers to contend with. Luckily, there are many ways to ward her off. Al Karisi is said to prefer sleeping victims, so one way to keep her at bay is to keep the new mother awake in the days after childbirth. The presence of a vigilant guard around the clock can help scare away any childbirth demons. In some traditions, Al Karisi will attempt to cross the first body of water she encounters after stealing a woman's organs—and once she does that, her victim is doomed to die. So if she has already managed to reach the victim, it is imperative to stop her from crossing water.

Other protections vary across cultures, including special prayers, charms, and apotropaic magic. For example, new mothers are sometimes encouraged to keep iron, onions, garlic, or knives on them at all times, especially when sleeping.

BABA YAGA

Slavic Witch of the Deep Forest

PRONUNCIATION: BA-ba YA-ga

AKA: Baba Jaga, Jaga Baba, Baba Roga, Ježibaba; meanings vary across the Slavic languages and cultures, but Baba Yaga's name can be broken down into two components: *baba*, meaning "grandmother," "old woman," or "hag," and *yaga*, meaning "witch," "spirit," "horror," "shudder," "anger," "fury," "wicked wood nymph," "serpent," or "snake"

APPEARANCE: Baba Yaga is sometimes an old woman and sometimes a trio of elderly sisters. She is described as hideous to behold—with iron teeth, a long nose, and spindly, bony legs.

SYMBOLS:

• **Chicken house:** Baba Yaga has an infamous sentient house that travels around the forest on chicken legs, never resting. The door is sometimes invisible, and the windows serve as eyes.

• **Mortar, kettle, or cauldron; pestle; and broom:** Baba Yaga flies through the air in a mortar, kettle, cauldron, or other vessels, using a pestle as a rudder. She also has a silver birch broom that she uses to wipe the tracks of her journey from the skies—making it impossible to find her.

Overview

Baba Yaga is a chaotic but neutral force in Slavic mythology. She is just as likely to help a hero or heroine as she is to hinder them. The earliest written account of Baba Yaga appears in 1755 in the *Rossiiskaia grammatika*, a book of Russian grammar. However, she had been featured in western Slavic oral folklore long before this time. She is often a bogeywoman used to scare children into behaving; her influence can be seen in characters such as the witch in "Hansel and Gretel."

In some stories, Baba Yaga asks heroes and heroines to perform a series of complex tasks to gain her favor (like separating grains of poppy seeds from soil or rotten corn from regular corn). If they fail in their tasks, Baba Yaga is happy to eat them—and she especially enjoys eating small children and babies. She grinds up their bones with her mortar and pestle.

She also has a flair for exterior design. She decorates the fence outside her house with the skulls of those unlucky enough to have crossed her, and there is always one post without a skull—where she can threaten to hang the heads of unlucky travelers or lost children if they displease her.

Baba Yaga often has helpers, including a traditional witch's cat and three mounted knights who represent the night, the dawn, and the sun.

In modern times, Baba Yaga appears in countless fairy tales and folklore collections, in the comics *Hellboy* and *Fables*, in the cartoon film *Bartok the Magnificent*, in *Dungeons & Dragons*, and even in the names of beers—a number of breweries have beers named for her.

What's Her Story?

One of Baba Yaga's most famous stories involves Vasilissa, a young girl whose father was a prosperous merchant. Vasilissa and her family were happy, until her mother became ill. When it became clear to her mother that she was dying, she called Vasilissa to her bedside and gave her a doll. She made

Vasilissa promise that she would tell no one about this doll and always keep it with her. Vasilissa promised.

After Vasilissa's mother died, her father decided to remarry. His new bride was a widow with two daughters of her own. At first, Vasilissa was excited to have a stepmother and stepsisters, but things soon took a dark turn.

Vasilissa was more beautiful than her sisters. And as she came of age, it was clear that people noticed. She got all the marriage offers, and her sisters got none. They were jealous, and so was Vasilissa's stepmother.

So when Vasilissa's father went out of town on business, his wife sold their house in town and moved the family deep into the forest. She knew that the forest was dangerous, and she was hoping that Vasilissa might meet with an unfortunate "accident"—or perhaps attract the malevolent attention of the witch of the forest, Baba Yaga. Then her own daughters would be free to marry without competition.

Vasilissa's stepmother constantly sent her on errands that took her deep into the forest and into Baba Yaga's territory. But Vasilissa always came back alive, and this became increasingly frustrating to the stepmother. So one day, Vasilissa's stepmother told her daughters to put out all the fires and candles in the house. Then she ordered Vasilissa to go and get a fire from Baba Yaga's home.

Vasilissa set out even deeper into the forest, where Baba Yaga was said to live. And, as always, she carried her trusty doll with her, the doll her mother had given her on her deathbed. Finally, the girl arrived at Baba Yaga's house—and she was not afraid. Unbeknownst to her stepmother and stepsisters, her doll had magical powers and had always helped Vasilissa complete her stepmother's tasks and stay out of the witch's clutches.

When Vasilissa arrived on Baba Yaga's threshold, the witch promised to help the girl if she could complete a series of impossible tasks. Vasilissa agreed, knowing that she had a secret weapon—her magical doll. Vasilissa completed all of Baba Yaga's tasks with the help of the magical doll, and the witch gave her the fire that she had requested in a skull lantern. When Vasilissa brought the fire back to her stepmother and sisters, it leaped from the lantern and burned them to death. They should have been careful what they wished for.

Vasilissa went on to live a long life and eventually married a prince—and Baba Yaga, as always, got the last laugh.

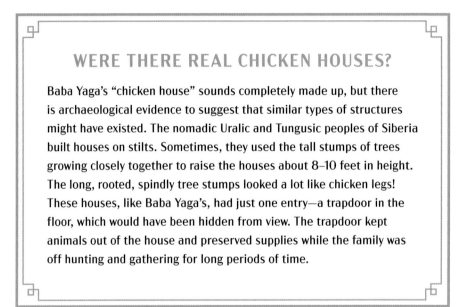

WERE THERE REAL CHICKEN HOUSES?

Baba Yaga's "chicken house" sounds completely made up, but there is archaeological evidence to suggest that similar types of structures might have existed. The nomadic Uralic and Tungusic peoples of Siberia built houses on stilts. Sometimes, they used the tall stumps of trees growing closely together to raise the houses about 8–10 feet in height. The long, rooted, spindly tree stumps looked a lot like chicken legs! These houses, like Baba Yaga's, had just one entry—a trapdoor in the floor, which would have been hidden from view. The trapdoor kept animals out of the house and preserved supplies while the family was off hunting and gathering for long periods of time.

BABAMIK

Cannibal Ogress of Papua New Guinea

PRONUNCIATION: ba-ba-MIK

AKA: Babamiku

APPEARANCE: Babamik is never physically described in any of her stories—except that she is an ogress and she can steal your skin and change her appearance to look like a human.

SYMBOLS:
• Crocodiles: Crocodiles are associated with Babamik, as she becomes one after her death.

Overview

Babamik is a terrifying cannibal ogress and adept hunter from Arapesh mythology. She has the ability to cause illness and death in humans and then take the skin of her victims. She uses this skin to impersonate the human she has killed.

Generally, ogres in Arapesh mythology can be either cannibals or vegetarians. Babamik, infamously, is a cannibal—and an extremely clever and successful one. She gets away with slaughtering her victims in public, without anyone else realizing what is going on. Her tale is a dark one, filled with baby eating, fishing, forbidden love, and a sinister take on motherhood.

What's Her Story?

One evening, Babamik heard two women down by the river. The women were both out at night, fishing by torchlight, carrying their infant children. Instantly ravenous, Babamik came up with a devious plan to satisfy her hunger.

The first step was to find a disguise. The next morning, Babamik came upon an old woman and spat on her, causing her to become ill and die. Babamik then stole her skin and put it on. Then Babamik caught up with the young mothers down by the river. The women had been cooking and making bread, and they offered some to Babamik, believing she was their mother-in-law, the woman Babamik had killed. Babamik offered to look after the babies while the women fished.

The women handed their babies over to Babamik. One was a baby boy and the other was a girl. Babamik strapped both of them to her and followed the women at a distance. Dropping farther and farther back, she began to enact her hideous plan.

She held the baby boy up and bit off one of his legs. The baby cried out, but Babamik soothed him. The women stopped fishing and asked if the baby was hurt. Babamik said it was just some bugs, but not to worry, she had shooed them away. The mothers continued fishing, and Babamik repeated this ploy again and again, eating the baby's other leg, then his stomach, head, and brains, until there was nothing left. Babamik then swaddled a log and put it into the sling in place of the baby.

The women finished fishing and asked Babamik to hand over their children so that they could feed them. Babamik handed over the baby girl and the log baby. The boy's mother quickly realized that this was not her child.

Surreptitiously, she warned the other mother that they had to flee— this was not their mother-in-law; this was an evil demon. Then she handed the log baby back to Babamik, pretending that she hadn't noticed and saying she would suckle the baby after she ate dinner.

Darkness fell. The moment Babamik's back was turned, the two women lit their torches and ran, fearing for their lives. In their panicked flight, they got caught up in some rattan plants, and the baby girl got hopelessly tangled. Unable to find her in the dark, the mothers were forced to abandon her.

Babamik came after the women and found the baby girl tangled in the rattan plants. But this time, she decided not to kill her. Instead, she adopted the baby as her own daughter. Babamik raised the child as if she were her own. Instead of feeding her human meat, she slaughtered a pig and fed her child pork every day. As the child grew, Babamik went out daily, slew a human and a pig, and brought them home for dinner.

The two lived happily together for a time, but as she grew up, Babamik's daughter slowly began to understand that there was something off about her mother's diet.

THE DEATH OF BABAMIK

As she grew older, Babamik's daughter began to wonder about the world outside her mother's home. She had spent all her life in Babamik's house, and she was lonely. The girl knew her mother loved her, but she had also realized long ago that her mother was a cannibalistic monster. One day, a young man visited Babamik's house and fell in love with the daughter. And the young woman loved him back. Day after day, the young lovers met in secret, careful to avoid Babamik's detection. Her sense of smell was excellent, and she could scent a human a long way off.

Babamik's daughter confessed to her lover that her mother was a cannibal and that she was terrified of what would happen when Babamik discovered that she had a boyfriend. So the boyfriend concocted a plan for them to run away together. He told Babamik's daughter to meet him at a certain spot by the river in five days, and the two fled across the river in a boat. But Babamik had caught the scent of "fresh meat" and realized that a human man had been near her home. She followed the scent and found her daughter and her lover fleeing across the river. Babamik called out to them, and they told her to follow by crossing a bridge made of logs.

But the bridge was a trap. The planks collapsed, and Babamik fell into the water, where she was clubbed to death by her daughter's lover. Before Babamik died, however, her spirit went into a crocodile. Babamik still haunts the banks of the river in crocodile form, looking for fresh meat.

CLÍDNA

Queen of the Banshees in Irish Legend

PRONUNCIATION: KLEE-na

AKA: Clíodhna, Clíona, Clíonadh, Clíodna, Clídhna, Clíodna of Carrigcleena

APPEARANCE: Clídna is said to be beautiful.
Some epithets refer to her as "the Shapely."

SYMBOLS:
• **Birds:** Clídna is said to have three bird companions with
bright plumage whose singing can heal the sick.

Overview

Clídna is a queen of the banshees in Irish folklore. (Read more about banshees in the following sidebar.) In some iterations, she is also believed to be a sea or water goddess, a goddess of beauty and love, and the patron goddess of County Cork, Ireland. There are many myths about Clídna, mostly centered around the area of County Cork. She is closely associated with an ancient Druidic tradition.

Her father is usually described as a powerful Druid—sometimes the last living Druid—and Clídna herself is said to be of the Tuatha dé Danann, a powerful race of fairies or supernatural people in Irish mythology. The Tuatha dé Danann may have been based on an ancient pantheon of gods once worshipped in pre-Christian Ireland. Their wisdom and magical skills also closely associate them with the Druidic tradition of the Celtic Iron Age.

What's Her Story?

Clídna's story is rather sad and tragic—as you might expect of a queen of the banshees. According to the story, Clídna was the daughter of the chief Druid of Manannán, king or guardian of the otherworld and god of the sea. She lived in the land of Tír Tairngire—or "the Land of Promise"—a sort of otherworldly spirit realm or paradise of the Tuatha dé Danann.

One day, a handsome adventurer named Ciabhán of the Curly Locks voyaged to Tír Tairngire to win her heart. He was good-looking and charming, and he won her over. Some versions say he kidnapped her.

Anyway, Ciabhán absconded with Clídna to the mortal world. On his way home, he left Clídna asleep on a beach while he went inland to hunt. While she slept, a great wave—sent by Manannán, who was mad that she'd left home—dragged her under the sea and drowned her.

The drowning was said to occur at a specific location in County Cork, Ireland: Glandore Harbour. (In some versions of the myth, the reason she falls asleep is because a musician from Glandore Harbour plays a soothing tune that lulls her to sleep.) This is why, to this day, the tide coming into Glandore Harbour is known as Tonn Chlíodhna, or "Clídna's Wave."

As for Clídna, she became a goddess of the sea after drowning in Glandore Harbour. She also, in some versions of the tale, returned to the realm of the Tuatha dé Danann and became queen of the banshees.

WHO ARE THE BANSHEES?

A banshee is a female spirit in Irish folklore whose presence foretells someone's death. She is known for her heartrending wail. A banshee usually predicts the death of a loved one or family member. The banshee does not lament just anyone's death; in some legends, she only appears for descendants of the most ancient family lines of Ireland—sometimes defined as those with a surname with an *Ó'*, *Mc*, or *Mac* prefix. Some banshees are attached to specific families.

Sometimes, a banshee appears to a family when their loved one is far away, and her appearance is the first notification they have of the person's death—in particular, she will appear as a young girl who has just died, to inform the family of the girl's death. At other times, the doomed person may spot her themselves as she washes their bloodstained clothes in the river. Often, the banshee appears to male warriors going to their death in battle. The banshee is closely associated with the Morrigan, who can also be spotted washing the clothes of the doomed at the fords. They may arise from the same ghostly tradition.

The word "banshee" comes from an Old Irish word that means "woman of the fairy mound." This ties the banshee to the Tuatha dé Danann, who were also said to live beneath ancient burial mounds from the Neolithic period that dotted the Irish landscape. Some legends associate Clídna's dwelling place with a rock formation named Carrigcleena, not far from the town of Mallow in County Cork, Ireland.

DEER WOMAN

Shape-Shifter and Protective Spirit
of Indigenous Women

AKA: Deer Lady

APPEARANCE: Deer Woman is a shape-shifter: She can appear as a beautiful woman with the hooves of a deer, an old woman, a white-tailed deer, or a woman from the waist up with the lower half of a deer.

SYMBOLS:

• **Deer:** Deer Woman is associated with white- and black-tailed deer.

Overview

Deer Woman appears in the stories of many different Indigenous peoples of North America, including the Lakota, Seminole, Pawnee, Oceti Sakowin, Ojibwe, Ponca, Omaha, Cherokee, Muscogee, Otoe, Iroquois, and Choctaw. According to some stories, she is a deer spirit associated with love, fertility, and the protection of women and children. To men who respect women and children, she is a benevolent force—but to those who harm them, she is a vengeful spirit.

Deer Woman often appears as a beautiful woman wearing a very long dress, and she tempts unfaithful men into the woods. How and where she targets these men can vary—sometimes she will find them by the road, at communal dances, or at communal events. Once Deer Woman has selected her target, she lures him away into the woods and then either tramples him to death with her hooved feet or enchants him so he wastes away from his love for her.

In popular culture, you can see the story of Deer Woman in the TV show *Reservation Dogs*. This modern interpretation of Deer Woman adds to the cultural canon of stories about her and shows how her myth has moved into the zeitgeist of twenty-first century Indigenous culture.

What's Her Story?

Deer Woman's origins vary greatly. According to some stories, she is a fertility spirit who looks after women during childbirth and promotes harmony and faithfulness in marriages. Some stories say that when you see Deer Woman, you are about to undergo a personal transformation. Others say that Deer Woman appears as a warning.

Most legends say that she is a spirit who watches over women and children and punishes unfaithful and dangerous men. According to some stories, Deer Woman was once a human woman who was raped and murdered, and she transformed into Deer Woman after her death to seek vengeance on men who prey on women.

Deer Woman can be seen at communal rites and dances; she loves to dance. She wears a very long dress—to hide her cloven feet—and is enchantingly beautiful. She finds her prey throughout the course of the evening and dances with him, talks to him, flirts with him—it all seems very normal. At the end of the evening, she tempts him to follow her into the woods, where he meets his grisly end. Deer Woman particularly targets young men, single or married.

Deer Woman is not a monster in the traditional sense. While she does some monstrous things, she does them for the protection of her community and her people. She does not feed on the souls or blood of the men she murders—rather, she can be seen as protecting women and the community from men who are unfaithful or predatory. Good men have nothing to fear from her.

While there is a tendency in some non-Indigenous Western sources to draw comparisons between Deer Woman and monsters like the sirens or succubi, these comparisons are superficial. Deer Woman's methods and reasons for her actions are very different from those of these monsters. Sirens and succubi feed off of men, any men, using their blood and bodies for sustenance. They are indiscriminate killers. Deer Woman is more of a protective spirit, targeting men who cheat on or abuse women and children. Her purpose is to keep women and children safe from men who would treat them badly.

Deer Woman has served as a cautionary tale to young men to beware of who they go home with. She is also a warning to men and women against promiscuity.

VIOLENCE AGAINST INDIGENOUS WOMEN IS STILL A SERIOUS PROBLEM

As a protective spirit who looks out for Indigenous women, Deer Woman is still very relevant today. Indigenous women are more than twice as likely to experience violence in their lifetime as any other minority in North America. According to multiple sources, one in three Indigenous women is likely to experience sexual assault, and 67 percent of these assaults will be committed by non-Indigenous people. They are also more likely to be victims of sex trafficking or murder, and these crimes often go unsolved. In 2021, the Biden administration created the Missing and Murdered Unit to help investigate crimes against Indigenous women. It is important to shed light on this violence and support the organizations that are working to help.

EL NADDĀHA

Lethal Temptress of the Nile

PRONUNCIATION: el nud-DAH-ha

AKA: En-Naddāha ("the Caller")

APPEARANCE: El Naddāha has been described as a tall, slender, beautiful woman with black hair hanging loose down her back. She may wear transparent clothes or be transparent herself. Few have ever gotten a good look at her and survived.

Overview

El Naddāha is a monster who stalks the banks of the Nile, luring men to their doom. It's not clear how old the myth of El Naddāha is. However, it's likely tales of her arose when the Nile was more rural than it is now. Many stories about her revolve around her targeting men walking along the riverbank alone, in isolated spots, or men who live in houses by the river in rural communities.

Descriptions of El Naddāha tend to be haunting and eerie. She's described as an impossibly beautiful woman—the better to stalk and beguile her prey—who is tall, slender, dark haired, and usually only glimpsed from a distance. The song she sings to lure her victims has a hypnotizing effect.

El Naddāha has become something of an urban legend in modern-day Egypt, where sightings of her are sometimes reported near the Nile. Stories about her are most common around the Nile delta north of Cairo, which tends to be more rural and agricultural. It's possible that her legend arose as a warning not to go near the banks of the Nile at night—where crocodiles, treacherous mudflats, and strong currents are all very real dangers.

What's Her Story?

According to legend, El Naddāha appears on the banks of the Nile to men walking by the river at night. She sings a bewitching, hypnotizing melody, rendering her target powerless to resist. Once she has removed her victim's will, she locks her arms around his neck and drags him down to the bottom of the Nile to drown.

El Naddāha sometimes takes a liking to her victims—and then it's even worse. If she falls in love with a man, she may take him back to her lair, an underwater cave full of treacherous currents. Once she gets him into her lair, El Naddāha will have sex with the man for weeks or months, keeping him bewitched and hypnotized. Once she tires of him, she will bury him alive in the floor of her cave and leave to continue the hunt.

Other times, El Naddāha is said to stalk men in their homes if they live in rural areas near the Nile. She has a slightly different hunting strategy then. Her song is said to be less enticing and more heartbreakingly sad. Her victim cannot run away from it, because El Naddāha knows where he lives. And as soon as he hears that song, the man goes into a distant, dreamlike state, unresponsive to his family and loved ones.

After a few days of listening to El Naddāha's song, the victim will sleepwalk out of his house and go to her on the banks of the Nile. She then drags him down under the water as she would with any other victim.

El Naddāha often targets men walking alone, but being in a group won't protect you. She's been known to pick out one victim from many, and when she does, there's nothing his friends can do to protect him. Legend says that if a man realizes his friend is being stalked by El Naddāha and tries to pull him out of her clutches, he will be her next target.

It's rare that anyone survives an encounter with El Naddāha. The only way to escape her alive is to avoid looking into her eyes. That's why descriptions of her are usually so vague—nobody who gets a good look at her is ever able to escape.

DJINNS OF THE NILE

Sometimes, Western sources link El Naddāha to sirens and other water spirits who lure men to their deaths with song. But it may be more appropriate to connect her to djinns. Djinns are supernatural beings or spirits from pre-Islamic Arabic mythology. They are neither good nor evil. They appear as benevolent forces in some folklore, but they can also be linked with demons and blamed for ill fortune, disease, and possession. El Naddāha is sometimes described as wearing a transparent dress or having an entirely transparent body. This could potentially also link her to djinns, which are sometimes described as having "subtle bodies"—in other words, not being entirely corporeal.

Like El Naddāha, djinns in pre-Islamic lore were also sometimes linked to mental illness. It's possible that myths of El Naddāha have been used to explain mental health conditions, including depression—especially when she hunted men inside their houses. Some myths about El Naddāha say that she drives men to suicide with her melancholy song. It's possible that her legend has been used to explain cases of suicide and otherwise unexplained changes in mental state in a time before modern psychology.

ISIQUQUMADEVU

All-Devouring River Monster of Zulu Legend

———————

PRONUNCIATION: ee-see-KO-KO-ma-DEH-vu

AKA: Usiququmadevu; name translates to "Smelly Whiskers"

APPEARANCE: Isiququmadevu is a fearsome monster, described as squatting, bloated, and bearded. In some descriptions, she's feathered; in others, she's hairless.

———————

Overview

Isiququmadevu is an all-devouring monster from Zulu mythology. She's described as both a mountain dweller and a river monster who swallows people, animals, and objects whole.

She is said to be constantly hungry, swallowing all living things she encounters whole. She has also been known to eat inanimate objects, such as clothes and jewels.

Isiququmadevu's story is similar to some others in folklore throughout Africa, in which a ravenous monster devours everyone in sight and a hero rescues them by cutting the monster open. Other examples include the

Kammapa of Sotho legend, the elephantine Liqimsa of Borana Oromo mythology, and the Dodo of the Hausa people (no relation to the extinct bird of the same name).

What's Her Story?

Legend has it that Isiququmadevu lived in the mythical Ilulange River. One day, the daughter of a king—Untombinde—decided to enjoy the river's natural beauty and go bathing in its pools. She took a group of approximately two hundred of her closest friends, which was not that unusual—princesses typically have an entourage.

Untombinde's parents had warned her of the danger. Everyone knew that the dreaded Isiququmadevu lurked in those waters, and nobody who went to that riverbank returned alive. But Untombinde was determined. She and her two hundred friends went down to the river, undressed, and left their clothes and valuables on the bank. Then they spent the afternoon playing and splashing and bathing.

They had a wonderful time. But when they came back to the riverbank, they discovered that their clothes and jewels were all gone—Isiququmadevu had stolen them while they were bathing.

The princess and her two hundred best friends were mortified. The girls went to Isiququmadevu and begged her to return their things, saying that it was all Untombinde's fault they were there in the first place—it was *her* idea to go to the river, after all.

One by one, the girls came to Isiququmadevu and begged her to give up their belongings. And one by one, Isiququmadevu vomited them up. But finally, when it was Untombinde's turn to ask nicely for Isiququmadevu to return her things, Untombinde refused. "I will *not* beseech Isiququmadevu," she declared.

So Isiququmadevu swallowed her up.

When Untombinde's father, King Usikulumi, heard what had happened, he was rightfully alarmed. He sent an army after Isiququmadevu, but she emerged from the river, opened her great mouth, and swallowed the entire army. And that was just the appetizer. Isiququmadevu then backtracked their trail to their village, opened up her great mouth, and swallowed up every man, woman, and child living there—as well as their pets and livestock.

A local man was returning from a hunting trip and saw Isiququmadevu devour his whole family—including his twin children. He vowed to rescue them. So he picked up his spear and went after her—but he quickly lost her trail. He refused to give up, however. The man kept going, encountering helpful animals along the way who pointed him in the right direction and offered encouragement.

Finally, he came upon Isiququmadevu herself. She imitated one of the encouraging animals, telling him that Isiququmadevu was just over the next hill and he should keep going. But the man was not fooled.

He took up his spear and stabbed her right in her bulbous hump, cutting her open. His family, the population of the village, and the king's entire army emerged from her body unscathed—followed by the haughty princess, Untombinde.

THE RIVER MONSTERS
OF SOUTH AFRICAN LEGEND

Stories of Isiququmadevu and varying water monsters of the Zulu, Xhosa, and other South African peoples have become the stuff of urban legends in modern times. For instance, in 1997, newspapers in South Africa reported sightings of a monstrous 20-foot-long reptile with a snake-like neck and the head of a horse, which was linked to the river goddess Mamlambo. Her victims were said to have had their brains sucked out of their heads. Approximately nine deaths in the area were blamed on the creature.

Another legendary river monster, the Inkanyamba, is said to live at the bottom of Howick Falls (known to the Zulu people as KwaNogqaza, or "Place of the Tall One"). The mysterious creature is said to drag people underwater and is sometimes blamed for violent storms and drownings. Like the Mamlambo, the Inkanyamba is said to be a serpentine creature with a horse-like head. It is most active in the summer months.

KITSUNE

Japanese Fox Demons

———◆———

PRONUNCIATION: kit-SOO-neh

APPEARANCE: Kitsune may appear as beautiful young women or girls, or as foxes. They also occasionally manifest as elderly men. In both fox and human form, the kitsune may have multiple tails—which they may or may not be able to hide.

SYMBOLS:
• **Foxes:** Kitsune are associated with many different types of foxes.

———◆———

Overview

Kitsune and other fox-like demons appear prominently in the mythologies of Japan, China, and Korea. In all of these countries, people lived side by side with foxes—both in rural and more urbanized areas. It's no wonder that legends developed around their presence. This entry focuses on the kitsune legends of Japan; this is not to say that similar creatures were not hugely important in other mythologies.

Japanese legend includes thirteen different types of kitsune. Each is associated with its own element or realm, including wind, fire, spirit, earth, rivers, oceans, mountains, forests, thunder, time, sound, the dark, and the heavens. While kitsune may appear as beautiful women or girls, they occasionally manifest as elderly men. As humans, kitsune have fox-like features, including narrow faces and sometimes fine hair on their bodies. They may also have a fox tail, or many tails, even when they appear as a human.

Depending on the age and power of the kitsune, they may be able to hide their fox tails when in human form—kitsune have multiple tails; the number of tails increases with age. In fox form, kitsune look like regular red foxes—except with multiple tails. Kitsune get another tail for every century they live, and at one thousand years old, their fox form is white with red-gold streaks—signifying their age.

Kitsune can be either benevolent or malevolent. These are considered *yōkai*, a category of Japanese demons. The benevolent ones, or *zenko*, are generally associated with the god Inari, and they are often depicted as white foxes with white tails. They protect communities against evil kitsune and evil spirits, and they are particularly fond of a fried, sliced tofu dish called *abura-age*.

The malevolent kitsune are called *nogitsune*. The *nogitsune* revel in tricking people and are particularly cruel. They target their victims by appealing to their worst vices—like greed, lust, pride, and vanity. They don't target women—their intended victims are men—but they do possess women and use them to lure their victims into traps.

In addition to being extremely long-lived, shape-shifting foxes, the kitsune have other magical powers, including the ability to create fires or wield lightning.

There is also a genre of folklore that concerns romantic relationships between kitsune and humans.

What's Their Story?

Perhaps the most famous kitsune story is that of Kuzunoha, and it is a romance between a shape-shifting fox spirit and a human guy. Kuzunoha was a white kitsune who fell in love with a mortal man. Her story comes to us from the tenth century A.D., and it is still told today through a number of Kabuki and Bunraku plays.

The story begins with Kuzunoha in her fox form, being chased by a hunter through the forest. In her flight, she came across a man named Yasuna, who was down on his luck. His father had lost most of their land and wealth to con men, and now he lived a meager existence. Kuzunoha, in her fox form, jumped into Yasuna's arms and begged him to help her. Yasuna agreed, for two very good reasons. First, this was a talking fox and it was definitely magical, and second, foxes were sacred animals, so he'd better just comply.

So Yasuna helped the fox escape. Thinking he had done his good deed for the day, he went back to his house, which he was rebuilding. However, the hunter had seen how Yasuna had helped the fox evade him, and he was enraged. He followed Yasuna and beat him up, leaving him badly wounded and unable to move.

After the hunter left, a beautiful woman appeared and began to tend to Yasuna's wounds. This was Kuzunoha in her human form, and she stayed to nurse Yasuna back to health. This took a while, and over the course of their time together, the two fell in love and got married.

Kuzunoha had a son with Yasuna, and for a while they were a normal, healthy family that seemed entirely human. But one day, when their son was five, he caught sight of his mother in her true form. Some legends say this was in a mirror, and others say that Kuzunoha, thinking her son was asleep, had transformed into her kitsune form.

With Kuzunoha's secret discovered, she had no choice but to leave her family. She ran away, leaving a note for her husband and child, telling them to meet her in the forest where the fox had first appeared to Yasuna.

Yasuna realized the truth—that his beloved wife was the same fox whose life he'd saved. He went out to see his wife one final time, and she bestowed magical gifts upon him and their son before she left her family and the world of humans behind forever.

KITSUNE AND KITSUNETSUKI

The kitsune were such a big part of Japanese culture that, as recently as the twentieth century, there was a form of mental illness believed to be caused by them. It was called kitsunetsuki. Kitsunetsuki was a form of fox-demon possession that happened to young women, and it was associated with fever. The fox demon was believed to enter the patient through her fingernails or breasts and possess her. This goes back to the ancient myths of the *nogitsune*, who possessed women and used them to entrap male victims. A woman who was suffering from kitsunetsuki might start to resemble a fox in her facial expressions, giving her face a narrow, fox-like cast. She might also spontaneously develop the ability to read, if she couldn't before. The only cure for kitsunetsuki was to undergo an exorcism at an Inari shrine.

KIYOHIME

Japanese Fire-Breathing Snake Demon

PRONUNCIATION: kee-yo-HEE-meh

AKA: Kiyo, Lady Kiyo, Princess Kiyo

APPEARANCE: Physical descriptions are very limited, but she is always described as a young woman—sometimes she is unmarried and sometimes she is a young widow.

SYMBOLS:

• Snakes and dragons: Kiyohime began her life as a human and then turned into a giant snake or fire-breathing dragon, depending on the version and translation.

Overview

Kiyohime is one of the most famous demons in Japanese literature. She is an example of a *honnari hannya*, a demon woman who has transformed into the strongest and most feared demon of all. But Kiyohime, much like other *hannya* (demon women), did not begin her life as a monster. *Hannya* are a type of *yokai*, or demon, in Japanese mythology that stem from human emotions. Many were once women whose hearts were broken by men and who were then consumed by intense rage, jealousy, or grief. Eventually, these women became *hannya*, vicious monsters intent on seeking revenge.

But the process did not occur overnight. It took a long time as the woman was eroded by her negative emotions.

There are three types of *hannya*. The least powerful have the potential to one day regain their humanity. The second-least powerful can also become human again, but only with the help of a Buddhist monk. The *honnari hannya*, the most powerful of the three, has completed her transformation—usually into the form of a snake or dragon—and she is beyond intervention. She will remain a demon until she dies.

What's Her Story?

The earliest mentions of Kiyohime occur in two collections of Japanese legends: the *Dainihonkoku Hokekyō Kenki*, which was written in A.D. 1040, and the *Konjaku Monogatarishū*, compiled in A.D. 1120.

There are many different versions of this tale. In one version, Kiyohime was a young girl who lived with her family in a prosperous manor house located on the pilgrimage route to a Shugendō shrine. Kiyohime's family opened their doors to the monks who passed through, making their annual pilgrimage. One day, they took in a handsome young monk named Anchin.

Kiyohime was a high-energy kid who was constantly getting into trouble. And the minute she laid eyes on the handsome monk, she developed a passionate crush on him. Anchin promised Kiyohime that if she behaved for her parents, then maybe he'd return to marry her when she was old enough.

Kiyohime held on to that promise. For years, she was on her best behavior, and she pined for the handsome monk, hoping every year that he'd stop at their home while on his pilgrimage. But he never did. He found other places to stay each time. When Anchin finally stopped at their home on his pilgrimage, he saw that she had come of age—she was now a beautiful woman. She reminded him of his promise to marry her. But instead of falling at her feet, Anchin was mortified. He told her he was just teasing her and trying to help her parents get her to behave. Kiyohime was shattered by his rejection.

On his way back from the pilgrimage, Anchin decided to take the long way around and avoid Kiyohime and her family's manor house. Kiyohime found out and was devastated. So she decided to leave home and track him down.

Realizing he was being chased, Anchin ran to the river, seeking to cross to the temple on the other side and ask for sanctuary. He managed to cross and then begged the ferryman not to go back and pick up Kiyohime. He knew she was following close behind.

But Kiyohime didn't need any help crossing the river. Her hurt and anger and rejection had transformed her into a *honnari hannya*—the most feared and powerful of demons. Normally these transformations took years, but this happened in minutes due to the ferocity of her pain. As she chased after him, barefoot, she started to shed her body and become a giant fire-breathing serpent—terrifying to behold. She swam across the river, undaunted by the swift currents. Meanwhile, Anchin only just beat her to the temple, where he begged the priests for sanctuary. They hid him in a large bronze *bonshō* bell, thinking he would be safe there.

But as soon as she arrived at the temple, Kiyohime caught Anchin's scent and tracked him to the bell. She wrapped herself around it and breathed fire on it, boiling Anchin alive as the bell melted around him. After she killed Anchin, she was so distraught that she drowned herself in the river.

There is a slightly happier postscript to this story. After his death, Anchin visited the dream of an elderly priest at the temple where he was murdered. Taking the form of a serpent, he told the priest that in this new life, he was now also a serpent, but he was not at peace. Kiyohime had followed him into this life as well. He begged the priest to perform a ceremony so that they could both be freed to reincarnate into different planes and lives. The priest did as Anchin asked, and both Anchin and Kiyohime finally found peace.

KIYOHIME IN NOH THEATER

The stories of Kiyohime and *hannya* are portrayed often in Noh theater. Noh theater is the oldest form of traditional Japanese theater still practiced today. It dates from around the fourteenth century, and it is still performed more or less unchanged from its original form. Noh theater often portrays a main character experiencing a single intense emotion, building that emotion through dance, gesture, music, and poetic recitation to reach an emotional climax. Many Noh plays end with a ghostly return to a significant place in the character's life, such as a battlefield or the setting of a passionate encounter.

Special masks, fittingly called *hannya* masks, were created to tell the story of *hannya* demons in Noh theater. They express the character's pain, rage, and despair as she transforms from a woman into a demon. The masks are carved from Japanese cypress and are beautifully painted and covered with a lacquer that can reflect light to subtly change the emotion being evoked. The masks tend to have a similar look: a square jaw, horns, a large sad smile that could be mistaken for a grimace, and shaggy black hair that represents madness.

LA LLORONA

Wailing Woman of Mexican Folklore

PRONUNCIATION: la yo-RO-na; la lo-RO-na

AKA: Weeping Woman, the Wailer

APPEARANCE: La Llorona appears wearing a long white dress and a white veil that obscures her face. Sometimes she is dripping wet, as if she has just risen from a lake or bathtub.

SYMBOLS:

• **Wailing:** A sure sign that La Llorona is near is the sound of a woman wailing—loud, heart-wrenching sobbing signifies her presence.

• **Water:** La Llorona is linked to bodies of water where she is said to have drowned her children. Water can be a sign that she is near.

Overview

La Llorona is a heartbreaking legend from Mexican and Southwestern mythology—a woman constantly tormented by the loss of her children. She is one of the most complicated figures in this collection.

Stories of her date back to the pre-Columbian colonization of the Americas. A weeping woman very similar to La Llorona is said to be one of ten omens that the Aztec people saw leading up to the siege of Tenochtitlán. She first appears in print in the 1500s in the *Florentine Codex*, a document written by a Spanish Franciscan friar, Bernardino de Sahagún. His interviews with Nahua people during the first decades of colonialism serve as a study, through a Spanish and Western lens, of the Nahua people.

In the codex, Sahagún recorded an account of the ten omens that heralded the brutal siege of Tenochtitlán by Hernán Cortés. The account is in Nahuatl, as described by Sahagún's Indigenous informants. Sahagún began this project in 1545—just twenty-four years after the siege of Tenochtitlán—so it is possible that some of his informants may have been survivors of the siege. The sixth of the ten omens was that of a weeping woman. She walked the streets of Tenochtitlán in the dead of night, weeping for her children and crying for them to flee the city.

Some historians believe that this figure was an early, pre-colonial version of La Llorona, connected to several Aztec goddesses. One is Ciuacoatl, a goddess of childbirth and the female equivalent of the feathered serpent god, Quetzalcóatl. She was said to appear at night, dressed in white, sometimes weeping or wailing. Her presence was said to be an omen of war. Another possible predecessor to La Llorona is Coatlicue, mother of the war god Huitzilopochtli. Coatlicue is said to weep as she waits for her son to return from war.

The third potential predecessor is Chalchiuhtlicue, an Aztec goddess of waterways, rivers, and lakes, who was said to overturn boats and drown people. This connection is particularly apt, because the city of Tenochtitlán was built on an artificial island in Lake Texcoco. Different areas of the city were bisected by canals and connected by causeways.

Chalchiuhtlicue's link to La Llorona is a dark one, because she demanded sacrifice. She was linked particularly to infanticide and the sacrifice of small children. Allegedly, the more a child screamed when they were taken from their mother to be drowned, the better the sacrifice would be.

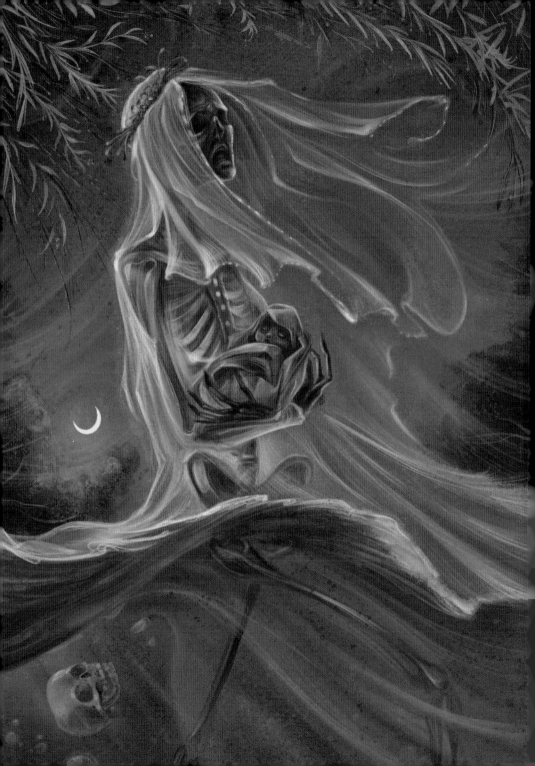

These are the ancient origins of the legend of La Llorona. In modern times, she has grown in mythic status, appearing in many films, novels, operas, and more. La Llorona appears in films such as *The Curse of La Llorona*; in TV shows such as *Supernatural*, *Grimm*, *Victor and Valentino*, and *Craig of the Creek*; in literature, including *Paola Santiago and the River of Tears* by Tehlor Kay Mejia, *The House of the Scorpion* by Nancy Farmer, and *Unconquered Spirits* by Josefina López; and in music and popular folk songs.

What's Her Story?

La Llorona's story varies greatly depending on the source and time period. But there are some recurring themes and details. One is that La Llorona is a grieving mother desperately searching for her children.

La Llorona's is a story of colonization and the stratified social order imposed on the Indigenous peoples of Mexico. She is often depicted as a young woman, possibly Indigenous, in a relationship with an aristocratic Spanish man. This difference in power and status between La Llorona and her lover is an important part of the story. Initially, however, the couple are happy together. They have children, and while they aren't married, their relationship is very much an open secret.

Eventually, the man's family decides that it is time for him to marry someone of his own social status—usually a daughter of the Spanish nobility. He marries in secret, but the news gets back to La Llorona. When he comes to see her next, it is to tell her that he can no longer be with her and that he wants to take their children to be raised by his new wife.

This story reflects an unfortunately common fate for Indigenous women during the colonization of Mexico, when Spanish men would sometimes take Indigenous women as wives or lovers and have children with them. But then they would remove the children from the mothers' care. This was done particularly for girls, because the colonizers believed that the Indigenous women would not be able to raise their daughters properly.

In myths about La Llorona, one of two things usually happens when the man attempts to take her children from her. In one version, La Llorona is so distraught that she kills her children on the spot. In the other, she has already drowned her children, and then, after this last meeting with her lover, she drowns herself.

But that's not the end of the story. The man is haunted by La Llorona and often does not survive long himself. In versions with a more overtly Christian message, La Llorona may be turned away from the gates of heaven because she has murdered her children. She is doomed to wander the earth, crying out for her lost children.

In modern folklore, she has become a bogeywoman parents use to get their children to behave. But her true tale is much darker and more tragic and reflects the brutality of colonialism and the experience of Indigenous women.

LA LLORONA AND THE DAY OF THE DEAD

La Llorona has become a part of the iconic Day of the Dead celebrations in Mexico, with some celebrants dressing as her in long white gowns and veils. It's traditional for plays and operas to run during the last two weeks in October in Mexico to coincide with the Day of the Dead—and La Llorona's story is a popular theme. While the origins of La Llorona's connection to the Day of the Dead are disputed, this connection is uniquely Mexican and shows the story of a people whose rich traditions stretch back through the ages.

LILITH

Bad Girl of Ancient Jewish Lore

———◆———

PRONUNCIATION: LIL-ith

AKA: Lamia (Latin)

APPEARANCE: Lilith has been depicted many different ways throughout the millennia. In some depictions, she's demonic and frightening; in others, she's a beautiful woman or half woman, half snake.

SYMBOLS:

• Owls: Lilith is associated with owls, and her name in some texts is sometimes translated as "Owl" or "Screech Owl."

• Snakes: Some believe that on the ceiling of the Sistine Chapel, the half-human, half-snake being coiled around the Tree of Knowledge in Michelangelo's *Fall of Man* is meant to represent Lilith.

———◆———

Overview

Lilith is a demoness from Jewish and ancient Mesopotamian lore. She appears in ancient Sumerian, Babylonian, Assyrian, Greek, Jewish, and Christian sources—she's even in the *Epic of Gilgamesh*. Lilith is sometimes referred to as "Lamia" in Latin; this version of her name appears in both

Latin and English versions of the Bible. The oldest depictions of Lilith are fragmentary and disputed. Ancient Mesopotamian cultures appear to have had a class of female demons called *liliths*, associated loosely with serpents, owls, and evil or diseased winds. Lilith also appears in a variety of Jewish texts, including the Talmud, Kabbalistic writings, and the Dead Sea Scrolls. She's mentioned in one line of the Hebrew Bible (Isaiah 34:14); her name was translated into "Lamia" in the Vulgate Latin version of the Bible in the fifth century A.D. and later carried over to English translations of the Bible.

In ancient Rome, people inscribed her name on ritual bowls and buried them beneath thresholds to keep out malicious spirits. They also wore amulets inscribed with her name, intended to stop her from doing evil to the wearer.

Lilith has been reclaimed in modern times as a feminist symbol—as the original independent woman who refused to submit to a man and was cast out of family life as a result. A prominent Jewish feminist magazine, *Lilith*, takes its name from her. Lilith and characters inspired by her have been depicted many times in popular culture, including in C.S. Lewis's Chronicles of Narnia, Neil Gaiman's *Sandman* comics, Cassandra Clare's Mortal Instruments series, Andrzej Sapkowski's The Witcher series, Qui Nguyen's play *She Kills Monsters*, and many other novels, plays, TV shows, movies, comics, and creative works.

What's Her Story?

Perhaps the most comprehensive myth about Lilith comes from the *Alphabet of Ben-Sira*, a satirical work in Hebrew. Its author is a mystery, and its dating is controversial. It may date anywhere from the 700s to the 1000s A.D. The *Alphabet of Ben-Sira* is not a religious text; in fact, it would probably have been seen as *very* edgy in its time. Its content includes references to masturbation, farting, incest, and heretical religious topics. It's here that Lilith is described as Adam's first wife.

In the story, shortly after God created Adam from the earth, he created a woman to be his companion—not from his rib, but from the earth in the same way Adam had been made. The name of Adam's companion was Lilith.

And as soon as God created her, she and Adam began to fight. The issue, as it is with so many couples, was sex. Adam was seriously vanilla—he *only* wanted to do it in missionary, and he wanted to be on top all the time. But Lilith refused to "lie below" Adam. They were equals, after all—they had both been created from the same earth.

Adam declared that she was *supposed* to be on the bottom because she was the inferior one; God clearly intended *him* to be superior. That, as you can imagine, did not go over well. Lilith dumped Adam and left the Garden of Eden, flying to a cave far away.

Adam prayed to God, complaining that Lilith had refused to submit to him. God sent three angels to go and retrieve her and promised Adam that if Lilith didn't agree to return, he would kill a hundred of her children every day.

The angels flew off in pursuit of Lilith. They found her in a sea cave overlooking the wild waters of the Red Sea, where she was busy copulating with demons and having demon babies, as one does. (Presumably, the demons let her be on top.) The angels told her that it was God's will that she go back to Adam, but Lilith refused to consign herself to an eternal wasteland of boring missionary sex. She adamantly refused to return.

The angels threatened to drown her in the sea. They threatened to kill a hundred of her demon babies every day. Lilith shrugged and said she would kill human babies in equal numbers, taking dominion over the first eight days of every baby boy's life and the first twenty days of each baby girl's.

The angels continued to threaten and harangue Lilith, and Lilith continued to dig in her heels. Finally, they agreed to let her stay and negotiated a deal in which they would leave her alone and she would not kill any babies wearing a protective amulet inscribed with one of the angels' names.

According to some versions of the tale, Lilith later attempted to return to the Garden of Eden, only to find that Adam had a new partner: Eve. In revenge, Lilith snuck into the Garden while Adam was sleeping and had sex with him while he slept, stealing his seed and later giving birth to a host of demons. In this way, she populated a demon army and became a demon queen.

LILITH AS FEMINIST ICON AND PATRIARCHAL SCAPEGOAT

The story of Lilith has been interpreted in many different ways. Some interpretations say she represents an ancient matriarchal tradition that was subjugated with the advent of agriculture and patriarchal religious beliefs. Through a feminist lens, she can be seen as the original strong, independent woman who refused to be dominated by a man. But in ancient Judaic and Mesopotamian mythology, she is generally presented as a destabilizing force. She seduces men and leads them astray; she kills women in childbirth and babies in the cradle; she threatens the family and the patriarchal order.

In some traditions, Lilith was blamed for stillbirths. Some interpretations of her story indicate she was blamed for wet dreams—as she was said to steal the seed of men while they slept.

MEDUSA

Misunderstood Monster of Greek Mythology

———◆———

PRONUNCIATION: me-DU-sa

AKA: Medousa, Medousê

APPEARANCE: According to some sources,
Medusa was once a beautiful woman, but she is most famous in her "monstrous"
form. Ancient writers tell us that her hair was made up of open-mouthed,
writhing snakes; she had wings, the tusks of a swine, flared nostrils, and a short,
coarse beard. In the later periods, Medusa is depicted as having a beautiful face,
hair of serpents, and the body of a snake. In mosaic art, it is common to see her
depicted with coiling snake hair and a pair of small wings on her brow.

SYMBOLS:
• Snakes: She is strongly associated with snakes.

———◆———

Overview

Medusa is one of the most fascinating and misunderstood "monsters" of
Greek mythology. The ancient Greeks and Romans retold her story with
fear and awe for the monstrous snake woman who could turn men to

stone with a single glance. They reproduced her fearsome image in artwork, talismans, and carvings on walls as a symbol of protection.

Medusa's story varies across the ancient sources, and some say she did not begin her life as a monster. According to some versions, Medusa's mother was also a half snake, half woman: Echidna. Her father was Typhon, a giant serpent. Together, Typhon and Echidna spawned most of the great monsters of Greek mythology, including Cerberus, the guard dog of Hades; the Hydra; the fire-breathing Chimera; and the Sphinx that terrorized Thebes—to name a few of their epic progeny.

Medusa famously had two sisters, Sthenno and Euryale. Together these women were called the Gorgons. Medusa's sisters are always described as monstrous from birth, with wings and snake hair. They are also immortal and ageless. But Medusa began her life as a beautiful mortal maiden, the only mortal in a family of monsters. Medusa continues to inspire countless books, movies, TV shows, artworks, poems, and video games. Good examples of retellings of her story are featured in Liv Albert's podcast *Let's Talk About Myths, Baby!* and Jessie Burton's *Medusa*. Avoid the remake of *Clash of the Titans*, as it does Medusa real dirty.

What's Her Story?

Medusa was a beautiful maiden with the most stunning hair; she lived at the edge of the world with her sisters. When she grew to adulthood, she decided to become a priestess of the virgin goddess Athena. She swore to live a chaste and virginal life in service to her goddess.

She would have been very happy living her life that way, if not for Poseidon. Zeus is famous for his many rapes and abductions, but his brother Poseidon was just as much of a predator. One day, Poseidon saw Medusa by the shore and decided that he had to have her. Medusa rejected Poseidon's advances, and when she realized that he wasn't going to accept her refusal, she fled to Athena's temple. She threw herself on the mercy of the goddess she had dedicated her life to.

But Poseidon didn't care that Medusa had sought sanctuary in Athena's temple. Poseidon and Athena had a rivalry that went back to the founding of Athens. So he followed Medusa back to Athena's temple and raped her.

Athena was so furious at what had happened that she "punished" Medusa by turning her into a grotesque and ugly monster. She cursed Medusa to have the tusks of a boar and hissing serpents for hair, and in some stories, she gave Medusa the body of a snake. Athena's curse made Medusa so hideous that no man could look at her and survive. Her merest glance turned men to stone.

There are some schools of thought that suggest that Athena's "curse" was actually a way for Medusa to protect herself from ever being assaulted by a man again. But another school of thought says that because Athena could not punish Poseidon for defiling her temple, she punished Medusa instead—in a terrible moment of rage and victim blaming.

There are no myths of Medusa behaving monstrously after her transformation. No stories tell of Medusa attacking villages or harassing humans. Instead, the legend tells us of a woman who was done with the world. She retired to a cave at the ends of the earth and wanted nothing more to do with humans. She hung out with her two immortal Gorgon sisters and waited for her death and an end to this curse.

But humans were not done with Medusa. As soon as news of her transformation from maiden to monster traveled across the ancient world, the "heroes" started arriving. One by one, these heroes, all men, attempted to try their luck slaying Medusa. And Medusa turned all of them to stone.

That all changed when Perseus showed up. Perseus was beloved by the gods, particularly by Athena. He was sent on a quest to bring back the head of Medusa as a wedding present for Polydectes. Several gods helped Perseus along the way—including Athena, who lent Perseus her polished, reflective bronze shield so he could avoid looking directly at Medusa; Hermes, who lent the hero his winged sandals; and Hades, who let Perseus borrow his helm of darkness.

With a lot of hand-holding and special equipment from the gods, Perseus was able to murder Medusa. He cut off her head, and from the drops of her blood sprang the winged horse Pegasus and the man Chrysaor. Both Pegasus and Chrysaor had been conceived when Poseidon raped Medusa and were born from her death.

WHAT BECAME OF MEDUSA'S HEAD?

After Medusa was beheaded, her severed head still retained its incredible power. The head was able to turn anyone who looked at it to stone. Stories say that even in death, Medusa's terrifying eyes remained open and the snakes of her hair still writhed, full of poison and malice.

There are many stories about what happened to Medusa's head after her murder. According to one, Perseus completed his quest and brought the head back to the ill-fated wedding, not as a gift but as a weapon. He used the head to turn the groom to stone. Perseus also used Medusa's head to rescue the princess Andromeda from the sea serpent Cetus. Then he married Andromeda and went on to found Mycenae, a major city in Greek mythology and ancient history.

Eventually, Perseus gave the head of Medusa to Athena as an offering and a gift of thanks for all her help in completing his quests. Athena added the head of Medusa to her shield, where it remains to this day, terrifying and frozen in horror.

PERCHTA

Yule Monster of the Alpine Mountains

PRONUNCIATION: PERK-ta

AKA: Percht, Berchta, Bertha, Perahta, Berchte, Frau Perchta,
Frau Faste ("the Lady of the Ember Days")

APPEARANCE: Perchta can appear as a young woman in white,
with skin and hair as white as the fallen snow. She can also appear as an old
woman—with a weathered and lined face, a beaked iron nose,
and an extra-large foot—wearing rags and carrying a cane.

Overview

Perchta is both an Alpine goddess and monster of Yule. She can appear as a young woman, fair as the freshly fallen snow, or as a terrifying old woman with a hidden knife—perfect for slitting open your belly. Perchta's story comes down to us through the oral traditions of Bavaria, Austria, and the Alpine regions. She is said to visit the earth during the Twelve Days of Christmas, from December 25 to January 6. In ancient pagan religions, this time of year was sacred because the veil between the worlds was thin. Mortals and immortals alike could easily cross the barrier between the land of the living and the land of the dead.

Perchta is also associated with the Norse holiday of Yule, a time when the Wild Hunt—a spectral hunting party of demons, gods and goddesses, and other mythical creatures—roamed the earth. Yuletide customs both celebrated the old year and ensured a happy and prosperous new year. However, these customs came into conflict with Christianity when it began to make inroads into the Alpine region.

With the advent of Christianity, figures like Perchta—with complex and nuanced aspects that included a dark side—were fully demonized, and their worship became forbidden. But that didn't stop people from worshipping her. And it doesn't keep people today from celebrating her during the Christmas season with parades and parties.

What's Her Story?

During the Twelve Days of Christmas, Perchta would ride through the skies with her Wild Hunt and visit homes around the countryside, doling out rewards and punishments to women and children. Perchta looked for industriousness and good behavior. A child who was well behaved and did all their chores would be rewarded with a silver coin in their shoe.

She was also a goddess of spinning and paid special attention to how productive women had been with their wool spinning. A woman who had a full basket of spun wool would also be rewarded with a nice silver coin. So would women who kept tidy homes, ate the right food, had well-behaved children, and left out nice plates of porridge for Perchta. They got to see Bright and Beautiful Perchta.

But those who transgressed would encounter the Ugly Perchta—and the punishments she meted out were severe. Perchta did not tolerate bad behavior, people who slacked on their work, or women who were anything less than domestic goddesses.

Women who failed to get all their spinning done before Yule—a time when spinning would traditionally be done for the year—could expect a visit from Ugly Perchta. Naughty children who didn't do their chores would find themselves on Ugly Perchta's list. If a woman's home was not clean and tidy, Perchta was ready to judge. Women who forgot to leave out bowls of porridge for Perchta during Yule would earn her enmity. And later, when Christianity began to overlap with older pagan cultures, women and children who ate anything except a meal of fish and gruel on her feast day (January 6—the feast of the Epiphany) would also get a visit from Ugly Perchta.

She would creep into her victims' houses at night, carrying her long knife. First, she'd trash the spinning room. Then she would slip into the bedroom while her victims were sleeping, slit open their bellies, remove their intestines, and fill them with straw or pebbles. Some stories say that she also set people on fire.

PERCHTA AND THE PERCHTEN

Perchta didn't go out alone during Yule. She had her own hunting party called the Perchten. The Perchten, much like Perchta, were dual natured. They could appear as bright and beautiful beings. In this form they were called Schönperchten, and they were said to bring good fortune and wealth to whomever they visited. But they could also appear as the Ugly Perchten, or Schiachperchten. These were creatures with fangs, horse tails, the bodies of goats, and huge tusks. They visited those who'd been naughty, and they were said to drive away evil spirits and demons. So, as much as they looked scary, they were also performing a service. They helped keep people safe from the darker creatures of the Wild Hunt.

The Schiachperchten looked a lot like modern depictions of Krampus. It is very probable that Krampus is directly descended from the Schiachperchten in appearance and inspired by Perchta in his deeds.

PESTA

Norwegian Spirit of the Black Death

———◆———

PRONUNCIATION: PES-ta

APPEARANCE: Pesta is described as pale and ashen faced, gaunt and elderly. She wears a red skirt and carries a rake or broom.

SYMBOLS:

• The color red: Pesta is said to wear red, which in Norwegian lore is associated with witchcraft, magic, and the supernatural.

• A broom and a rake: Pesta is seen carrying one or both of these with her at all times. If she is carrying a broom, everyone in a village will die; if she carries a rake, only some will die.

———◆———

Overview

Pesta is a terrifying spirit who is said to personify the Black Death in Norway. She is often described as an ashen-faced elderly woman, sometimes blind, who carried the disease to communities throughout the country. The Black Death came to Norway in 1349, and within a year it had killed a large percentage of the population. The exact number is disputed, but it may have killed as many as two people out of every three.

Stories of Pesta often depict her in a haunting landscape of lonely valleys, high mountains and forests, and echoing fjords—the iconic topography of Norway, now emptied of people. During the Black Death, entire villages were abandoned; bears hibernated in empty churches; isolated survivors walked pathways they'd traveled all their lives, spotting corpses in the undergrowth as the forests slowly reclaimed the roads.

This image of Pesta walking alone probably describes a familiar sight in Norway at the time—evoking the terrifying loneliness and enormous grief of a population ravaged and a landscape emptied out by plague.

Interest in Pesta revived in the 1800s with the publication of Andreas Faye's collection of Norwegian folklore in 1833 that featured stories of her. In the late 1800s and early 1900s, the Norwegian artist Theodor Kittelsen made a series of illustrations of Pesta that captured her haunting, grief-stricken iconography. In more modern times, Pesta was featured in the video game *The Witcher 3: Wild Hunt*.

What's Her Story?

Pesta is described as a lone elderly woman wearing a red skirt, bent-backed and carrying a rake and a broom that she uses to sweep the landscape clean of human habitation. If she carries a rake to a town, some will survive; if she carries a broom, all will die. Everywhere she passes, people die in droves, leaving the land to the beasts and the supernatural creatures of the forests and underworld and the howling wind coming off the sea.

Pesta moves from village to village and home to home, often traveling by boat across the fjords to reach isolated communities. One myth tells of a boatman who picked up an old woman traveling from one village to another across a fjord. As he rowed her across the deep, narrow lake, the boatman slowly realized who his passenger was. Stopping in the middle of the fjord, he begged her to spare his life. Pesta told him that she could not protect him from death, but she could make his end a peaceful one. The man returned home feeling slightly sleepy. He lay down on his bed and fell asleep; by morning, he was dead.

Tales of Pesta illustrate the way the plague behaved and spread. Her stories show us how closely and accurately the Norwegians observed the disease, even without the benefit of modern medical knowledge. Like Pesta, the plague moved from village to village and from home to home. It traversed vast forests and mountain ranges, even crossing water. Pesta is often depicted as traveling by boat, with the unlucky boatmen dying soon after they transport their deathly passenger.

In reality, the bacterium that caused the Black Death—*Yersinia pestis*—often came to communities by boat, carried both by infected people and rats. In Norway, where long, deep, and narrow fjords score the landscape, boat was often the only way to travel between isolated villages.

A GHOST SHIP RUNS AGROUND

The way the Black Death came to Norway is especially spooky. In the fourteenth century, the plague spread through Europe, traveling from east to west on merchant ships. As news of the plague spread, countries started to restrict travel and quarantine foreign merchant ships to prevent the disease from entering. It didn't work. The plague continued to spread, primarily on those merchant ships.

In 1349, a merchant ship sailed from England to Norway with the plague on board. Some stories say that the crew tried unsuccessfully to contain the disease by quarantining sick sailors, but it didn't work. One by one, the crew members died—until finally the ship ran aground on a beach near Bergen, with all or most of the crew dead on board.

This account is disputed, however. Other accounts state that the crew was not all or even mostly dead by the time the ship arrived in Bergen, but they started to die soon after the cargo was unloaded—and then the population of Bergen started to die as well. The inhabitants of Bergen sank the original merchant ship, but by then it was too late. Accounts also tell of several other ships running aground on beaches in the area, with all or most of their crews dead, as the disease continued to burn through Europe.

THE QALUPALIK

Inuit Sea Spirit Who Lures Children Onto the Ice

PRONUNCIATION: the ka-LOO-pa-leek

AKA: Qallupilluit

APPEARANCE: There are conflicting accounts about the Qalupalik's appearance.
Generally, she is described as having scaly green skin, webbed and
clawed hands, and a frightening appearance.

Overview

The Qalupalik is a sea-dwelling spirit in Inuit mythology who lures children to their deaths out on the sea ice. Accounts of her appearance vary, but she is generally described as a frightening sea creature, perhaps humanoid, with a gaunt face and sunken eyes, green skin, inhumanly long fingernails, and long dark hair. She may also have some fishlike features, such as scales, fins, or webbed fingers and feet. Her face may appear rotting and bloated, like that of a drowning victim. Some legends say she smells of sulfur.

The Qalupalik is said to carry an *amautik*, a traditional parka with a special built-in pouch to carry a baby. The *amautik* is traditionally worn by Inuit women, and the Qalupalik wears one to carry stolen children.

The Qalupalik is featured in several children's books, including *A Promise Is a Promise* by Robert Munsch and Michael Kusugak, and *Putuguq and Kublu and the Qalupalik!* by Roselynn Akulukjuk and Danny Christopher.

What's Her Story?

Like many legends, the story of the Qalupalik bears a warning for children: Stay away from treacherous ice. The Qalupalik is often depicted as preying on children alone or in pairs, and separated from adults. This carries another warning for kids growing up in an environment with a lot of dangers: Don't stray too far from your parents or a trusted adult.

According to the mythology, the Qalupalik's hunting grounds are Arctic shorelines and ice floes near the shore. She waits for children to wander nearby, and when they do, she emits an ethereal, irresistible hum that lures them farther out onto thin, dangerous ice. Some legends say that the Qalupalik waits near holes in the ice, listening for children to wander too close so she can drag them down into the frigid water. She may even knock on the ice to draw her prey farther out onto unsound ice.

Once she has caught a child, the Qalupalik may devour or drown them, depending on the legend. However, frequently it's said that she keeps them alive but in a sleeping state, draining their life and energy to keep herself young and preserve her long, flowing hair. Thus, children stolen by the Qalupalik are kept forever in a kind of half-waking state, in the cold and far from their families and communities.

But not all children are lost completely when captured by the Qalupalik. Some legends feature kids who get rescued or outsmart her. In one story, a woman and her grandson lived in a small hut by the sea. They were poor and had no kin, and the child cried because he was hungry. The grandmother had no way to feed him and believed he would surely starve if he stayed with her. So she took the child to the icy shore and called upon the Qalupalik to come and take him.

The Qalupalik emerged from the sea, scooped up the child, and put him in her *amautik*. Then she disappeared beneath the waves. Not long after, some hunters in the grandmother's community had a streak of good luck. They brought in a great deal of meat and blubber and shared some with the elderly woman. She lamented giving her grandson to the Qalupalik, because now she had enough to feed him.

A young couple overheard her story and promised to rescue the boy. Both the man and woman were talented hunters. They knew that to catch elusive prey, they had to be patient and watch carefully. So they went out onto the ice, and they watched. Eventually, they noticed that where the tide rose and fell, it created deep cracks in the ice. The couple could see the child deep in the cracks, playing with a strand of seaweed. The Qalupalik had tied the boy to the seaweed so he wouldn't drift away. The couple tried to reach the child, but as soon as he saw them coming, he sang a song of warning. The Qalupalik pulled the seaweed and drew him back beneath the waves.

The Inuit couple embodied patience. They were quiet as could be, but the child always detected them coming, and the Qalupalik always pulled him back under the waves. Finally, they concealed themselves and waited by the crack all night until the sun came up. When the child first appeared in the crack in the ice, they cut the seaweed and snatched him out of the sea.

LEARNING FROM ICE IN THE ARCTIC

For generations, Inuit people have passed down time-tested techniques for moving across ice safely by foot, via dogsled, or on snowmobiles. However, global warming has changed conditions so drastically that some of this ancient knowledge no longer applies. As global warming makes the ice more treacherous each year, the Qalupalik's warning grows more and more important.

RESOURCES

Al-Ayad, Djibril, and Valeria Vitale. *Fae Visions of the Mediterranean: An Anthology of Horrors and Wonders of the Sea.* Futurefire.net Publishing, 2016.

Albert, Liv. *Greek Mythology: The Gods, Goddesses, and Heroes Handbook.* Avon, MA: Adams Media, 2021.

Bane, Theresa. *Encyclopedia of Beasts and Monsters in Myth, Legend and Folklore.* Jefferson, NC: McFarland, 2016.

Bassett, Molly H. *The Fate of Earthly Things: Aztec Gods and God-Bodies.* Austin, TX: University of Texas Press, 2015.

Bierhorst, John, trans. *History and Mythology of the Aztecs: The Codex Chimalpopoca.* Tucson, AZ: University of Arizona Press, 1992.

Breckin, Edmund. *Frau Perchta: The Christmas Belly Slitter: A Concise History of the Festive Legend.* Independently published, 2017.

Canizares, Raul. *Oya: Santeria and the Orisha of the Winds.* Farmingdale, NY: Original Publications, 2006.

Davies, Sioned, trans. *The Mabinogion.* Oxford World's Classics illustrated ed. Oxford: Oxford University Press, 2008.

Dharma, Krishna. *Mahabharata: The Greatest Spiritual Epic of All Time.* San Rafael, CA: Mandala Publishing, 2020.

Eagle Walking Turtle. *Full Moon Stories: Thirteen Native American Legends.* New York: Disney Hyperion, 1997.

Foster, Michael Dylan. *The Book of Yōkai: Mysterious Creatures of Japanese Folklore.* Oakland, CA: University of California Press, 2015.

Hayes, Joe. *La Llorona / The Weeping Woman: An Hispanic Legend Told in Spanish and English.* El Paso, TX: Cinco Puntos Press, 2006.

Hubbs, Joanna. *Mother Russia: The Feminine Myth in Russian Culture.* Bloomington, IN: Indiana University Press, 1993

Ihimaera, Witi. *Navigating the Stars: Māori Creation Myths.* Auckland: Penguin Random House New Zealand, 2020.

Illes, Judika. *Encyclopedia of Spirits: The Ultimate Guide to the Magic of Fairies, Genies, Demons, Ghosts, Gods & Goddesses.* San Francisco: HarperOne, 2009.

Jackson, Lesley. *Isis: Eternal Goddess of Egypt and Rome.* London: Avalonia, 2016.

Kinsella, Thomas, trans. *The Táin: From the Irish Epic Táin Bó Cuailnge.* Oxford: Oxford University Press, 2002.

Kwa, Shiamin, and Wilt L. Idema, trans. and eds. *Mulan: Five Versions of a Classic Chinese Legend, with Related Texts.* Indianapolis: Hackett Publishing Company, 2010.

LeCapois, Teejay. *The Vampires of Somalia: Modern Somali Mythology.* Lulu Press, 2021.

Lie, Jonas. *Weird Tales from Northern Seas: Norwegian Legends.* Iowa City, IA: Penfield Books, 2008.

Lindow, John. *Norse Mythology: A Guide to the Gods, Heroes, Rituals, and Beliefs.* Oxford: Oxford University Press, 2002.

Luo, Liang. *The Global White Snake.* Ann Arbor, MI: University of Michigan Press, 2021.

Mahdi, Muhsin. *The Thousand and One Nights.* Leiden, Netherlands: Brill, 1995.

Malory, Thomas. *Tales of King Arthur & the Knights of the Round Table.* London: Flame Tree Collections, 2017.

Mama Zogbé. *Mami Wata: Africa's Ancient God/dess Unveiled.* Vol. 1. Independently published, 2007.

Mohamed, Farah M. *The Somali Queen: Queen Arraweelo.* Alexandria, VA: Somali Media Company, 2014.

Mohanty, Seema. *The Book of Kali.* London: Penguin Books, 2009.

Monaghan, Patricia. *The Encyclopedia of Celtic Mythology and Folklore.* New York: Facts on File, 2003.

Ngọc, Hữu. *Viet Nam: Tradition and Change.* Athens, OH: Ohio University Press, 2016.

Nimmo, H. Arlo. *Pele, Volcano Goddess of Hawai'i: A History.* Jefferson, NC: McFarland, 2011.

Nozaki, Kiyoshi. *Kitsune: Japan's Fox of Mystery, Romance & Humour.* Stone Bridge Classics, 2008.

Oswalt, Wendell H. *This Land Was Theirs: A Study of Native North Americans*. 9th ed. Oxford: Oxford University Press, 2008.

Ovid. *Heroides*. Penguin Classics ed. Translated by Harold Isbell. London: Penguin Books, 1990.

Ovid. *Metamorphoses: A New Verse Translation*. Penguin Classics ed. Translated by David Raeburn. London: Penguin Books, 2004.

Pae-gang, Hwang. *Korean Myths and Folk Legends*. Fremont, CA: Jain Publishing, 2006.

Pryke, Louise M. *Ishtar*. London: Routledge, 2017.

Qitsualik-Tinsley, Rachel. *The Shadows That Rush Past: A Collection of Frightening Inuit Folktales*. Iqaluit, Nunavut: Inhabit Media, 2018.

Roberts, Ellie Mackin. *Heroines of Olympus: The Women of Greek Mythology*. London: Welbeck Publishing, 2020.

Schwartz, Howard. *Tree of Souls: The Mythology of Judaism*. Oxford: Oxford University Press, 2007.

Takruri, Akan. *100 African Religions Before Slavery and Colonization*. Jamal White, 2017.

Teixidor, Javier. *The Pantheon of Palmyra*. Leiden, Netherlands: Brill, 1979.

Weber, Courtney. *The Morrigan: Celtic Goddess of Magick and Might*. Newburyport, MA: Weiser Books, 2019.

INDEX

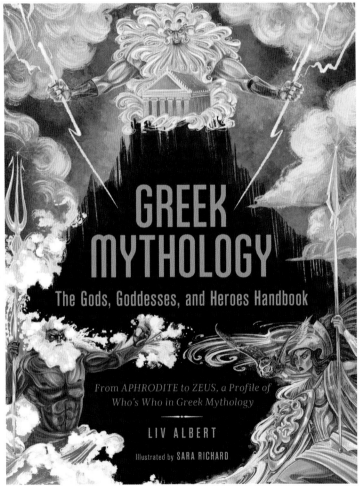